Thresholds

Near-Life Experiences

Edited
by
Gabriel Bradford Millar

Hawthorn Press

Contents

'The Light, the Light! The Heart-Delighting Light!'[1]

Crossing

Deliverance

[1] Lord Byron

Dedication verse

Past the impasse, you showed me —
The dragon in the foreground,
And the castle ahead —
And no way but past him, into
His belly, Parsifal

Wear the old skin, until it
Cracks open — and the blackness
Breaks to gold: was that it?
Yes: and I am that salmon
You saw, swimming upwater

And as gold as the Word is
In Love, and fire, and water
There is only the source
And the river — only the sky
And the upstream — forever.

Arc of unending Light.

— Jay Ramsay

Foreword
by
Sir George Trevelyan

Breakdown, break-up, break-in, break-out... such is the nature of our tumultuous age as seen by the rational mind that still conceives matter to be the primary reality. But the final epithet: BREAK-THROUGH — this is what begins to happen now, as we realize that beyond matter are primary realms, finer and subtler, reaching on and up into Life, Light and Spirit. Breaking through the barrier is a vital event and phenomenon of our time, through which we recover the lost truth that all the visible world is a reflection of a primal creative field of Spirit. As Goethe wrote in the closing lines of Faust: *All that is transitory is but a parable.*

Now in our time, when Planet Earth faces much destruction through human greed and folly, there begin to be ever more frequent examples of sudden breakthrough into a higher vision, glimpses of hidden reality bringing wonder and joy. This may well be the prelude to a true change in consciousness, the experiencing of the reality of higher worlds which we are called on and entitled to explore. We get glimpses through the veil. Beyond fear or frustration is the great hope of redemption.

More and more people are being given the break-through experience in consciousness, the sudden vision of a greater reality which underlies and overlights our death-ridden physical world. Then we achieve the vital certainty that the human being is in essence a divine spiritual entity, immortal and imperishable, housed in the transitory temple of a mortal body, which enables us to operate as free spiritual beings in the heavy density of the material world. Earth is then seen as the training school for eternal souls. The goal, indeed, appears to be the evolving of the individual soul to freedom as a conscious co-creator with God. Once we really see this, life takes on new meaning and purpose.

Our Editor has had the enterprise to collect a number of descriptions of these break-through experiences, which will bring excitement and hope to many. *So it is true, what I have dreamt, glimpsed and hoped!* A start has been made in exploring this remarkable phenomenon. It may be hoped that this book will encourage others who have recorded such experiences to send them in to the Editor so that a further volume may be published. Here is a field of research of eminent worth and interest, and its theme is of first importance as we break through into the wider vision of the Aquarian Age.

Prologue

This book is born into a time when more and more people are experiencing a dimension in their lives that is of a different order, and has a different charge, from their daily, pragmatic awareness. Unexpected rescue (in psychic and physical crisis), consolation, insight and direction come from this other dimension.

These experiences are often fleeting and unsustainable, and more intimate than romantic love, almost too intimate to talk about.

The aim of this gathering of accounts is to convey, through personal testimony, moments or events that have signalled a chance for profound change. These are as unique as the individuals who experience them. It is a book of common revelation, written by a cross section of people, some illustrious and some obscure.

My heartiest hope for this book is that it will prompt in you, the reader, a respect for the authority of your own inner experiences, and the realisation that this rich inner domain is not the exclusive province of mystics and saints.

We are familiar with the phenomenon of the near-death meeting with a spiritual being. Reports of these stem from the 1930's and the traumas of World War II. With the rise of the Third Reich and the epitome of evil, came a new power of the soul to perceive the fact that, on an inner plane, we are accompanied, consoled, championed and inspired. Stories of supersensible strength and forgiveness came out of the camps of both Hitler and Stalin. Researchers such as Elisabeth Kubler-Ross and Jacques Lusseyrand have recorded them. Dr. Bernard Lievegoed, head of the Dutch army's psychiatric unit in 1939-40 describes the time he was trying to fetch food for the Zonnehuis children's home in the 1944 'hunger winter' in Holland:-

'With a cart through the snow, fetching potatoes in Utrecht, miles and miles, hoping the Germans wouldn't catch you, the cold sweat in your shoes.... I know what it means to be a fugitive, to have no food. You know what it is with war? You get to live totally in the outside world. You live from one day to the next. For me at least, I did not lead an inner life, my inner biography in a certain way seemed to have stopped. I was completely oriented to the outer life.

During the war, on top of everything else, we had a scarlet fever epidemic. Fortunately, all the children pulled through, but the consequence was that I got it myself almost a year later. I was very ill, had all kinds of complications such as erysipelas and kidney problems, fever above 106 degrees. But I lay in bed singing, felt great and thought that everyone was worrying about me without reason. Everyone was afraid I would die. But I experienced all sorts of things on that sickbed. One of those things has remained very important to me for the rest of my life.

At the crisis point of the illness I had certain visions. I witnessed what was happening in Russia. And I kept hearing a voice that said: battle of Uman, battle of Uman.... What I experienced was the retreat of the German troops across an endless plain, troops that went through the landscape in irregular groups without formation. Then appeared a peasant's cart pulled by a horse in which there was a young German soldier, dying. I saw at that moment what the soldier was experiencing: from the distance a figure approached him who waded through the landscape the way you wade through water. A great figure of light. When this figure had come very close the boy died. I experienced this picture so strongly that it stayed with me the whole time and I have often thought: you did not experience that for nothing. In my feeling I have often connected the picture of the dying soldier with the well-known words 'In Christo morimur... In Christ we die...' Since then it may really be said, I know what happens when we die. You must remember that I was also standing at the edge.

from ***The Eye of the Needle*** by
Bernard Lievegoed, Hawthorn Press 1993

Raymond Moody has since documented many death experiences. The thrust of this book is that we do not need to be near death to have threshold experiences: the sharers in this book affirm that we can have glimpses of eternity in the midst of temporal life.

The issue of death was taboo during the prosperous years of this century, and the logical intellect of our time has not been comfortable with experiences that are not induced by drugs. Now these taboos are lifting, as we become more and more willing, even in science, to explore a realm beyond the one circumscribed by the literal mind.

Since the Renaissance we have been plummeting into matter. Self-exiled from our origins, mesmerized by matter, armoured against each other, we wither and get ill. And because there is fear where there could be love, we do gross things to each other. We are a death-dealing culture; the media purveys death and we buy it. "The price of distance is death." (Jay Ramsay). We have turned away from Life, and will go on until it becomes bitter and unbearable — for some it is already unbearable.

Especially this century we feel the godforsakenness Parsifal felt —

the cost of choosing non-relationship. We have had to estrange ourselves to be free. With our free will we can choose, like Parsifal, to be safe instead of saved. But this safety is *papier-mâché*; anything can poke holes in it: frustration, accidents, loss, illness or death.

With the same free will we can turn towards Life, so that It may find entrance and ground in us.

On September 20, 1990, Sergei Prokofieff, grandson of the composer, spoke in Stourbridge. He said that because of our closed, myopic thoughts, spiritual beings see a dark abyss when they look at the earth. This abyss is punctuated by points of light emanating from those whose thinking is not materialistic; these appear like stars in a dark sky. He said that mankind has now crossed the threshold, but is still largely unconscious of it.

On this brink of a new millennium, more and more of us know moments of unprecedented openness when light enters, love ignites, and our lives shift into a new vector. The Epiphany in 30 A.D. in the river Jordan was the incorporation of the highest Presence into the earthly Jesus.

Epiphanies is a gathering of accounts of flashes across the line between the sensible and the supersensible. There are now more and more conscious crossings. We cannot yet sustain what we discover there, but "In these matters to know once is to know for ever" (Kathleen Raine).

Contributors were asked to describe a time of total clarity, or a moment when the heart spontaneously opened, or a point of contact with their deep will to be born. The outcome is 38 accounts across the social and professional spectrum.

Epiphanies

I am a threshold child: I merely point to It. I live in the longing to give entrance and ground to the Divine. I can do it only sometimes.

My life rehearses the swerveless gesture of pointing to the possibility of starting heaven here. I practise helping people remember their source — I can do it only by remembering mine.

Like John the Baptist, I am an only child. Like many only children, I am a child of older parents: my father was 68 when I was born, and my mother 33. I have always wanted to do more than survive the malady of the day, and to offer something incorruptible, to point to epiphanies. Often I am dismayed by my ordinariness...
but there are epiphanies.

— Gabriel Bradford Millar

'Us the most fleeting of all'
— Rilke 'The Ninth Elegy'
Duino Elegies

Meeting

John Gale

The son of an Anglican clergyman, John Gale spent his childhood in Norfolk. At the age of 18 he became a Roman Catholic and lived for 12 years as a Benedictine monk. Since leaving monastic life and the priesthood, he has lived in London where he works as a psychotherapist. He is married to an Argentinian and has published research on the psychological aspects of primitive monastic teaching and practice. He describes himself as a 'Catholic agnostic'.

The Meeting in the Café

Despite the fact that it tasted rough to my throat, I accepted another Gauloise and ordered an expresso. It was like a kind of hysteria. We were laughing and talking all at once, unable to stop. Contact had been difficult in the monastery. I used to be so envious of Harry. He seemed to have an interior discipline I could never discover for myself. It was something intangible but very powerful. I was very hungry for something like that. But the deeper inside I turned, the more I just stumbled on disquiet, uncertainty and an immense emptiness. Harry seemed centred and sure of himself. Only later was I to sense that this too was a defense against the intolerable pain of our situation. For the moment, though, some of the desperate despair was lifting and the contact and intimacy of this meeting — brief but intense — was making me get back in touch with myself and find my centre and my core once again.

It had been a good three months since I had seen him and he looked so different and cool and normal in his blue suit. The cropped monastic haircut had almost grown out and he looked like he blended well here. The coffee was strong, like him. Black, simple, without compromise. I looked at myself and felt flabby in my cast off clerical suit and I wanted to have the security Harry seemed to have. I wanted to be sitting on his side of the table. We were talking about commitment. Not about commitment to an ideal but to a process, the inexorable internal journey that paces itself at a very individual rhythm. Commitment to the unrelenting, unyielding demand to grow, change, develop and to own oneself as process. Yet it was not just what we were saying, but that was part of it too. So was the washed out look of the young man behind the bar and the weary eyes of the secretary sitting at the next table. It was the whole package. I gradually became aware of the background music, a Charlie Parker trumpet and piano pushing, stretching notes and beat just that bit further than one might expect. It was not exactly Gregorian chant but it had the freshness and intensity of a sequence and it had the same effect, that mixture of placid insistence, urgency and depth which formed the backdrop and pulse of each day over the last twelve or so years of cenobitic life. With every blast I felt a surge of energy, mind and spirit, tensing and releasing something inside me. Suddenly I knew that this moment was not just another antiphon. It was a crisis. A rupture.

The monastic rhetoric had begun to sound sour over the last year since the canonical Visitation when all my hopes for renewal within the community had been dashed. Some years before I had begun to question certain attitudes in the community. At that time, reformation was almost non-existent. The novice master was rather frail and did not like controversy or discussion. Consequently, there was practically no intellectual or theological content to the novitiate programme. The abbot was clearly coming to the end of his period in office and his chapter sermons reflected this fact. And so I became critical of the general lack of awareness and lack of direction which resulted from this situation.

In contrast, the student master was a sharp and original thinker and, as a student, I discovered the historical and intellectual perspective which my previous criticism lacked. This was especially true of monastic history. I began to feel that the community had come to an impasse. On the one hand, there were those who advocated renewal. But this group seemed simply to want a relaxation of discipline in order to do their own thing. On the other hand, the traditionalists looked back, not to the primitive inspiration of the earliest monks, but rather to the romantic revival. I had wanted to find a way out of this dilemma. I soon discovered that I was driven by a desire to realize a more radical alternative to the complacent mediocrity of the institution.

I began to articulate what I had already sensed some years earlier through my work teaching the student monks, through my sermons to the community, my voice in the abbot's council and in chapter. But most especially in my relationship with the new abbot. But as the years progressed, I began to be more and more frustrated as both the abbot and the community seemed almost totally absorbed with the concern for economic security, ecclesiastical status and its own image. Unwilling to take any risks. Primitive monasticism, in contrast to this, had in part been a protest against a bourgeois and worldly church. It had been a life of struggle, a resistant. We didn't seem to be resisting anything or protesting. There was nothing marginal about us and we were not on any frontiers. The monastic institution seemed to be providing security rather than enabling the process of self awareness. Mind you, there was a lot of rhetoric.

Harry wasn't giving me any rhetoric. He was just telling it how it was. There was a need to work, a demand to take a stance, a set of relationships to find, build, create. There was this café, this blue suit. He seemed to have killed off Descartes once and for all. "The monism of the phenomenon rules, O.K.!" Sartre would have liked Harry.

Suddenly I saw the possibility of a life without the necessity of the hidden worlds-behind-the-scenes scenario. Suddenly the scent of freedom. The freedom to let go of the killing burden to be special. Liberation into a single dimension. It seemed so zen. So monastic. A paradoxical smell of fresh air after the stale heavy atmosphere that had so far lasted a lifetime. There seemed a possibility to be ordinary.

At that moment, a girl squeezed past our table. She was in her late teens. Her blue dress clung to her body and ended just above the knee. Her body was strong and muscular without any unnecessary fat. She seemed perfect. Integrated. At home with her sexuality, magnetic and powerful yet quite without tension. I wondered if a day would come when I would feel one dimensional and able to be totally present to a woman's body, at home with my response. Free from the guilt I now felt and which internally had begun to censure my curiosity and attention.

All the monastic arguments against leaving seemed to have dissolved. Leaving was clearly not giving way to temptation or 'giving up the fight'. It would be a damned hard move away from a cosy environment where status and material security were assured regardless of performance. Harry was underlining this. It was no longer an academic or theological point. It was a reality. The question now was whether or not I would ever have the guts to test myself in the market place.

I thought of the chant. Back home in the monastery there was this endless chant. It was a paradigm of monastic life. Monotonous, warm, endless, quite effortless and tranquil. It seemed to put me in touch with myself and gave meaning to every aspect of my daily experience. The psalms. Monotony, repetition. I knew that nobody who had not experienced monastic life would ever fully understand me. Part of me would always feel like a stranger, an outsider, a foreigner. It had been a whole culture. An entire unconscious formation. There would always be a permanent nostalgia. Hearing the loud silences, saying mass alone on cold winter mornings. Bowing in white woollen cowls, hands on our knees. Chopping wood during manual labour and nodding off during lectio as the dawn rose. *Plenitudo legis est dilectio!* Some moments would never be forgotten and the resonance of those experiences would cause goose pimples to stand up on my arms, sitting in the back of the nave of a monastic church in France, on casual visits, for years to come. It had been so good. So intense. But there was now the possibility of a new future. I knew now that it was my fate. That it would be desperately difficult to turn my back on my brothers who may never understand, but that it was the only way forward. I had to be true to myself.

I felt alone as Harry said goodbye and as if I was at a kind of crossroads. As I brushed past the crowds of workers in the underground I felt less out of place. I had already begun to face a new direction.

The air was cool and I turned up the collar of my jacket and sensed that my melancholic expression went unnoticed in the anonymity of the crowd. I knew that nothing would ever be the same again, but that any future would be one I helped create for myself.

— John Gale
Ex-Benedictine Monk/Priest

Sandra E. Westlake

I was born on the 29th of March 1940 into a large gregarious family of five girls and two boys.

Educated at Stroud High School, I left in 1951 and worked for some years as a stable-girl.

My hobbies are walking, gardening and reading – especially poetry.

One Day

About eight years ago, I began work in a new office. My mother had recently died, and I was feeling very low in spirit.

One day a delightful young lady came to my till and presented her child benefit book to me, on the cover of which were written these words:

If you keep a green bough in your heart,
the singing bird will come.

I felt transformed. My spirit lifted instantly. The proverb was so apt, the words so beautiful, and the promise of hope and optimism I drew from it lifted my flagging spirit and gave me a fresh outlook on life.

I try now to keep this thought in my mind and to use it as my philosophy of life. And I find I am better able to cope with outside pressures when I remember "the singing bird will come".

— Sandra Westlake
Teller, Stroud Post Office

Richard Wainwright

Richard lives in London. He is a poet, teacher and therapist, combining several disciplines in his work. He is a senior lecturer in Dramatherapy at St. Albans School of Art and Design (Univ. of Herts), with specialisms in physical theatre, voice work and the linkage between archetypal psychology and theatre practice.

He is an analytically trained counsellor and therapist with a particular interest in all forms of poetics, verbal and non-verbal.

Herne Sense

I was recovering from a minor operation that had developed complications when I left London with my wife and children to join some of the other members of our family for a holiday on the Isle of Mull. The debilitating effects of anaesthetic had been compounded by a mild infection, neutralised by a stringent dose of antibiotics. I was permanently exhausted and our journey left me feeling little more than a shapeless sack of toxin, drained of body and soul, utterly self-enclosed.

I couldn't or wouldn't be restored by the natural relief of arrival that lifted everyone to jubilant enthusiasm, opening into wonder at the magnificence of so many meetings of land, sea and sky. I tried, blankly, to go through the motions, but enthusiasm, born in the moment of arrival, springs from a generous release of life. I remained crabby and withdrawn, despite some muffled pleasure at the spaciousness and beauty of the house we were to stay in. It was sheltered in the embrace of a curving throne of hills and looked outwards to Carsaig Bay and a sullen sea of pewter. At last I could retire and go to bed.

Mull and Iona are defined by absence; the absence of a screen that separates you from what you see. I have never known light to have such depth, for even at its brightest, it is in touch with something soft. Here, seeing is a matter of being touched with sight and informed with a sense of the world seeing through itself in dreams of colour in shadow and light. Seeing the shake of cloud shock in shadows scudding across richly piled emerald hills, or jewelled blue water, you can feel their lightening and darkening spreading and locating new perspectives in deeply woven patterns inside your eyes, and the colour of depth is blue.

Ultimately, the aliveness and intensity, the mood and tone of every colour suggests a mode of blue. Colours play into each other in waves. They don't lack definition, far from it, but the definition is always moving, re-defining not just what you see, but how you see what you see. Landscape is no longer entirely solid, nor water liquid. The skin, that usually separates imagination from the world in our part of the world, thins and almost dissolves.

The earth clothed in colour by the artifice of light turns wonder into form, exposing nakedness of feeling in emotion. Love, grief and fear are recombined in a perpetual sense of immanence. It runs deep in the chest and diaphragm opening, expiring and trembling with inspiration of when the world was new. Only when the earth moves through your feet lightly are you held in step by gravity. Without the rain here, human life would be impossible. It rains a lot.

After four weeks of blue green shadow play and silver leap in the heart of deep drum chest, feeling full and at the same time utterly empty, I left the house alone and in the evening to walk. Feeling such aliveness in being alive now flowed into feeling abandoned where the flow of feeling thickened, seized by sadness which hardened into violent, undifferentiated grief. What had been unlived or put away was reawakened. It was the pain that comes when the grace of fullness reconnects with the bitterness of limitation. All my good weather was gone. I felt poisoned by bad faith.

A hint of moonlight, touching the hill I was climbing, relieved the pressure of churlish rage and drew me ahead of myself. To the left a steeply banked wood, mainly pines, intensified the darkness in which I could just distinguish a thick jungle of fern. I kept an eye on the moonlight gathering at the top of the hill, while looking repeatedly into the wood, vaguely stirred by the sense of being watched that comes from darkness.

Out of the trees and at the crest of the hill, I was free, alone. The moon was rising to its fullness. Away to the right the sea shimmered in swathes of shaken silver, and the hills ghosting the bay were stained like ancient blackboards. I noticed the harbour, its great luminous stones crumbling into the sea, but I still remained attached somewhere to the residue of the mood that had engulfed me when I began to walk. That mood of self recrimination and resentment gathered again and broke across this almost unbearable luminosity that filtered into memories of other places I had loved, or been loved by, that would not be left behind and could not be recovered. Out of this sense of loss, sullen waves of anguish rose with a fervour that felt crushingly familiar.

There is a feeling of deep disgrace in the bitterness invoked by rabid recollection of disappointment. Even though I could see the futility of resentment, I couldn't see through it and there was no shaking it off by act of will alone, no voluntary submission to the spirit of Ash Wednesday. I could not, or would not give up the hope "to turn again", feeling compelled to trawl through the ashes of exhausted, or unrealised hopes and ambitions, unaware of the fear in my rage at having to let go.

The moon had risen above the trees when I moved back down the lane towards the house. Shadows had fallen across the road. I peered at rather than into the wood, now on my right and thicker than before; looked away, behind and up at the moon for reassurance. What had stirred before and stayed inside was now palpable. I turned to the moon and span, heart drumming and head jerked round in wild arrest.

Something huge in startled cavort; frenzy breaking unformed out of darkness. I, an inblort of terror, strained for clarity, but not wanting to see the blort of monster bulge careering in the dark and near, near enough to be everywhere. *I*, not existing, had disappeared in nameless dread.

The swirling, cavorting and tearing suddenly ceased. Standing clear and bold in the moonlight was a stag, a few feet away, still and staring at me. We stood looking at each other, neither moving. Gradually the terror subsided. As it drained away, the fixed stare loosened; I noticed some fern dripping from one of his antlers. He inclined his head towards the sea and we moved away from each other. Touched by the slightest stirring of the breeze, I realised my face was wet and streaming still.

When I got back, the gate, posted against a huge copper beech, was already open. The air was filled with the roar of waterfall and I, shocked from bitterness dissolved, felt blessed; blessed with the gift of Herne sense and knew that it could not and would not belong to me alone.

Epilogue

The following night my brother-in-law came to me: "Come and look," he said softly. He led me with my wife to his room and pointed to the window. "Look out there." Once again the bay was cast in silver. My eye settled on the riot of fuschia in the garden; clear red at night. "Can you see them?"

"Yes, they're so red," I said dumbly. "No, over there," whispered my wife, nudging me and pointing to the space between the garden and the sea. Thirty or forty deer were stirring in the park beyond the garden. They had come down to drink where the river, fed by the waterfall, runs into the sea.

The three of us stood in silence, contained in a single smile; the kind that looks outwards, reflecting a smile.

— Richard Wainwright
Therapist

Leslie Kenton

Award-winning writer, television broadcaster and author of numerous best-sellers, **Leslie Kenton** is described by the press as 'the most
original voice in health' and 'the guru of health and fitness'. She is
well known for her no-nonsense approach to teaching and highly
respected for her thorough reporting. In recent years her work has
been increasingly concerned not only with the process of expanding
individual health but of helping herself and others re-establish deep
bonds of connectedness with the earth as part of healing the planet.
Health Editor for *Harpers and Queen* for fourteen years, she has been
a consultant to Britain's *Open University* and to medical corporations
in the United States. She won the 1984 PPA *Technical Writer of the
Year* and her work has been honoured by her being asked to deliver
the McCarrison Lecture at the Royal Society of Medicine. In 1988 she
received the *Gordon Whitehead Award* for her work.

All I Ever Wanted Was a Baby

"Please tell me again. Please tell all of it from the beginning. Please, please," I begged my mother as she straightened the seam in her stocking and zipped her dress. She picked up a heavy comb and dragged it harshly through her long blond hair. "But I've told you, Leslie, a dozen times. You don't want me to go through it all again, do you?" "Oh yes, please, just *once* more," I cooed, with all the charm a four-year old could muster. My mother sighed, glanced at her watch and, I suspect, wondered how she'd explain to my father *this time* why she'd taken so long to dress. Then she began again...

An age-old scene, you may be thinking. The child begs for the same fairy tale. The good-natured parent tells, yet again, how the funny-looking duckling turned into a beautiful swan. But this time things were different. For the fairy tale I begged for was nothing of the kind. I was asking my mother to tell me the *real* story of how babies are born.

As far back as I can remember, all I really ever wanted was to have a child. Oh, don't get me wrong. I was never taken with ideas of sweet little things wrapped in pink or blue — far from it. I thought the traditional image of mother and baby looking longingly into one another's eyes was sappy and sentimental. This desire for a child, which first came at the age of three or four, was far more basic than that. I never played 'house' with any of my friends, and I gave away every doll I ever owned because I found them so boring. Instead, I played football with boys, climbed mountains, swam. Yet, somewhere deep inside me, a quiet voice told me that the key to everything lay in fulfilling some kind of impelling biological purpose in my body — giving birth.

Luckily, I had a mother who believed in being truthful. She told me all the facts — from the mating of animals and a man and woman, to the seed in the womb and the birth itself. Each time I listened, enraptured with the story, although she never embellished a thing. She never spoke about love, or tenderness. It was always very clinical — vagina, afterbirth, intercourse — and yet, to me, the magic was there.

It may seem strange that a small child could have such ideas, but I did. Whenever I broached the subject, whether with my friends or with adults (which I couldn't resist doing), my excitement was met with disbelief, even shock: "Now, my dear, don't you worry your head about such things, go out and play for a while." Like a cat who proudly drags his trophy — a bloody mouse — into the house to show the family, only to find he is met with horror and shoved quickly out the door again, I soon learned to keep my opinions to myself. I locked my joy and the desire for a baby inside my most secret heart and there, for years, it stayed. I never told another living soul.

After all, what nonsense. I came from a 'progressive' family where girls were taught that they were just as good as boys and were brought up to make their own successful way in the world. *They* told me I was supposed to be bright, attractive, educated, and, above all, successful. I wasn't to think about foolish things any more, *they* said. Of course I wanted to become an important grown-up like *them*. So, I decided, if that was what the grown-up world was all about, then that was what I'd become.

The years passed. I studied all the adult games hard and learned them well. The way to say good morning, how to argue a point and still seem intelligent, how to be hypocritically polite to people I couldn't stand. I was determined to do it all right. Yet it soon became obvious — when I was around sixteen or seventeen years old — that something was missing. I had done all they asked of me, I'd been a good girl, now where was my reward? It never came. I found I was disappointed with this wonderful adult world I had been so carefully prepared for. It left me with a certain emptiness inside. If the truth be told, I was miserable. I hid the misery, knowing that hiding unhappiness was one of the most important rules of being accepted in this strange world to which I somehow didn't seem to belong. But when I was alone, the emptiness gnawed at me.

So I drank a little too much, went to as many parties as I could (the louder the music, the better), drove my car a bit too fast; and, after I entered university, didn't bother to sleep much either. I was reckless and careless about myself, but cheerful, hard-working and successful in the face I showed to the world.

Sometimes, at night, I would drive to the sea and watch the water sloshing back and forth against the rocks and I'd wonder why I didn't just walk into the waves and drown. Perhaps, I thought, that would bring me the sense of excitement or knowledge that everything was more than just the empty game that life seemed to me. Perhaps then I'd understand what it was all about, I thought. Then, I'd remember my wish for a child, the way you discover some lovely trinket in a forgotten drawer, and instead of dramatically heading into the water, I'd drive quietly home and go to bed.

Strange, perhaps, but I never considered getting married. I knew well that one needed a man to have a child. And, for that matter, I liked men. I just never longed for the ring and the white dress.

The time arrived. I was in university. I'd met a young medical student who was strong-willed, upstanding and sincere, and we became lovers. Within a few months I was pregnant.

"You're pregnant?"

"Yes."

"Are you sure?"

"I'm sure."

"But how can you know. It's only been three weeks."

"I just know. I feel *different* inside."

And different I felt all through. Inexplicably, the sense of emptiness which I'd come to believe was my birthright as an adult ebbed away... not that it was no longer there, but it now seemed unimportant, irrelevant. The empty girl, who drove too fast and slept too little, rapidly became the defender of life within her body. "I'm sorry," I'd say to anyone driving more than fifty miles an hour, "I don't mean to be a nuisance, but would you mind driving more slowly, please. You see, I'm *pregnant*."

Pregnant. Even the sound of the word had a certain magic to it. There was life inside me, not only the baby's life, but my own, and I couldn't risk letting anything happen to it. Suddenly my body was geared to something *real* and there was no mistake about it.

Two months later I wrote a letter:

Dear Father, I'm pregnant. I know it may come as a shock to you. But I am very happy about it and hope in time you will be, too. I have no intention of giving up the baby or of having an abortion. He is to be born sometime in January. I will have to take a term off from university to have him and then I'll go back to my studies. I hope you are well, and I send my love, Leslie.

My poor father was, quite understandably, horrified. He found my whole attitude far too unconventional. He wrote back saying that there was no possibility of my being a *mother* without being a *wife*, too. Either I got married or I gave up the baby. I was taken aback, even somewhat crushed by his attitude, and what I saw as his lack of understanding. But, being an obedient child, I did what he asked. Luckily the young man was willing, even eager. So married I became, complete with the white dress and all the trimmings and trappings.

Four months later, one winter afternoon in a huge teaching hospital, our child was born. The labour was long and, regrettably, not

15

'natural'. I was given an analgesic during labour and a spinal block for the delivery. It was all very cold, very efficient and very mechanical, yet my mysterious passion for birth remained undaunted. For the first three days after he was born, I sat up in bed unable to sleep with excitement. "My God, isn't it fantastic; isn't it fantastic", I repeated again and again under my breath.

My child was immediately taken from me and put into a nursery with all the other babies while I was wheeled off to a private room. Soon they brought this tiny creature to me. I held him in my arms and stared at him with stark wonder. Then, at three-hourly intervals, he would reappear for twenty minutes at a time and I'd hold him in bed beside me until the nurse would come and take him away again. The third or fourth time they brought him to me, he began to cry. I nestled him. I rocked him. I spoke gently to him, but he wouldn't stop. I rang for the nurse.

"He's crying," I said. "What should I do?"
"Have you burped him?"
"No."
"You *have* fed him, of course."
"Fed him? Am I supposed to feed him?"

I was in a Catholic hospital where most of the women were having their third, fifth, even ninth baby. No one had considered that I might not know what to do!

The nurse took him and put him to my breast. His tiny mouth opened and reached for me as if he had known forever what to do. He began to suck with such force it took my breath away. It was like being attached to a vacuum cleaner. I began to laugh. I couldn't help myself. It seemed incredible that such a tiny creature could have such force and determination. He too had a purpose. He was raw, insistent and real. With every fibre of his being, this child was drawing his life. And he would not be denied.

Tears of joy ran shamelessly down my cheeks while he sucked. I thought back to the story that so many years before had delighted me, and to the certain conviction I'd had that only when I had a baby would I *know* whatever it was I had to know. Now I *did* know. It is the only important thing I have ever learned, and so ridiculously simple: Love exists. It's real and honest and unbelievably solid in a world where far too much is complex and confusing and false.

There, in the midst of all that clinical green and white, I had discovered what love was all about. It was a meeting of two beings. The age, the sex, the relationship didn't matter. That day, two creatures — he and I — had met. We touched each other, in utter honesty and simplicity. There was nothing romantic or solemn about it. No obligations, no duties, no fancy games. We'd met. Just that. Somewhere in spirit we were friends. I knew beyond all doubt that I'd found something *real*. And real it has remained.

Now my eldest child is nineteen and it is a long time since that first day when I held him, not knowing what I should do next. Somehow, we would find what to do and what to say to one another. It was only a question of being still enough to listen to each other, and having faith. That faith has never left me. Love exists... real love... not the kind that depends on who you are or how you look or whether or not you are kind to someone. This meeting — this sharing — this naked confrontation where two beings are, for an instant, together. Now I could live with all the fancy adult games and be indifferent to them. I would always be able to bear the feeling of emptiness that sometimes comes. For I knew that someday, sometime, this *meeting* would come again with others — and it has.

— Leslie Kenton
Nutritionist

Alan Jackson

I'm still here, and the story represents what happened to me over a period of time.

The Birth of Nilus Absinthe

Nilus Absinthe sat at his desk, smoking, sipping, mulling over the plot of his next naughty epic of murder, sex, and imperial intrigue. Where would he set it? What names, what twists, what auras could he have in it? Above all, what could he have in it that was new? That would make a slogan, make a poster, make the millions pay millions? As part of his mind slipped in and out of eras and galaxies, another part wandered and began to compose something for his present self.

What if, as he sat there, a modern man about his natural business of accumulation, a presence appeared and stood behind him, so awesome, so powerful, beyond anything known, that when he turned round and saw it, he would feel a fear and a loosening, fall from his chair to the carpet and cry out in a scream: "No, no, my God, no."

The figure was dark, yet with rippling lights in it, that wavered in and out of a human shape, about eight feet high. Nilus was half propped against his desk, his mind bursting with terror, looking up at it, stammering "wh..." sounds: "Who, what, where?"

— Stop it, Nilus, stop it. The voice was very deep like a crack in the ground, and it was totally and utterly penetrating and effective.

Nilus stopped and became empty dead clear.

— Sit on your chair, light a cigarette, turn round to face me, and listen.

Then Nilus was looking at this colossal fact and sat like a stone and waited. One puff, two puffs, three, and the figure spoke.

— You are Nilus. You are a wretch, a traitor, an ignoramus, a creator, an artist, a wealthy man. You are famous, you are a fool. You are a prince of your profession, you are a pervert. You are nothing, you are a pawn, you are a pinch of dust. You are a heretic, a rebel and a mercenary. You are a winner of awards, you are welcome everywhere, you are a whore. Your life up to this moment has been worse than worthless. What you see before you is the accumulation of your thoughts, deeds, and inventions. And I am hellish, terrible, and merciless. And I am real. For the first time in your life, Nilus, you are seeing something real.

The voice was deep, clear, and chilling as ice. Nilus fainted.

19

— Wake up Nilus.

Nilus woke, and looked again. He had no doubt this was real and his terror was total. He thought...

— You want to ask who I am?

— Yes.

— The present content of your mind can't receive my name. What you need to know is this. Your life is entirely in my hands. In this second, I can cancel your contract if I wish. Do you understand?

Nilus understood. In his whole life there had never been anything like this, and he knew he was nothing.

— Now this is the purpose of my appearance. After your years of fantasy and crime, both on the screen and in your life, I have come to bring you your reality, the reality you have accumulated. You are going to take part in a monstrous, filthy, and wicked murder.

— But I don't want anything like that. Why should I want that?

— But you will, Nilus.

— Why, for God's sake, why?

— Because all your life you have dreamed of these things, and worse – you have taken your dreams, and expanded them, and embellished. You have studied literature and art and history and technique in order to improve and perfect them. And then, Nilus, you have sold them.

— Shit, that was just entertainment.

— There is no such thing as entertainment, Nilus. There is only truth and untruth, love and hate.

— But it's an escape valve, it helps people let off steam.

— No, Nilus, it does not. It perverts their minds and inflames their passions; it loosens their hold on the day to day and increases their susceptibility to darkness. This is not a dead world, though you have acted as if it was. It is a totally living infinite interconnected universe, with no inside or outside but all whole now always; and every thought, every wish, every image, has an effect and reaches out and touches others and makes the sum of things either better or worse, lighter or darker.

— But I didn't know this. I just...

— No, you didn't know it, or at least you ended up not knowing it, but you could have. You chose not to, you chose not to care. You have reached tens of millions of beings with your entertainments of lust, power, blood and witchcraft. You have added to their isolation, their despair, their self-involved imagination. You have fed their secret selves on darkness.

— Well, they didn't have to, did they?

— That's true. But it is your life I have in my hand at the moment, not theirs. And you did what you did consciously, at the height of your ability and that is why you are receiving this confrontation. You expended a great deal of energy in a certain direction. You cannot escape the ray that returns. You studied every means available to make them come and watch; you examined trends, statistics, other successes. You knew that what was forbidden was what was attractive and so that was what you gave, deliberately. And as with the years society changed and what had the taste of 'forbidden' had to become worse and darker and more evil you followed, without second thoughts, because for you it meant fame, power, money, and women.

And the higher you rose the more you despised the people you claim to have been entertaining. You called them suckers, Nilus, but if what they were sucking at was you, then who or what have you been?

Now the time has come for you to pay. The machinery has been set in operation, the set has been ordered, the script commissioned, the actors engaged, the plot has begun. You are going to take part in an abominable crime.

If there can be ice within ice then Nilus was pierced even deeper. He shook his head.

— It is true. It is truer than anything you have ever thought or said.

— Wait, wait, I mean apart from.. what you said, what have I actually done to deserve this? I've never actually hurt anybody.

— You mean you haven't cut little bits off people with a knife, or poisoned them, or laughed as soldiers pierced children with spears from horseback. But you have cut a little bit off every woman you have had sex with, and they are many. You have poisoned to a degree everyone who has had contact with your degenerate mind. You have fathered several children to whom you have never given anything but cheques and expensive toys. You are a skunk, and now you are going to pay. You have twenty four hours to decide.

— To decide? To decide what? You mean I've got a choice?

21

— The forces that have been set in motion are still not absolutely defined. There will be a crime of a shattering and degrading kind, but you have a choice...

— C'mon, tell me. What is it?

Nilus was hopeful. Maybe this was just a lesson. The figure waited to give Nilus a chance to expand his hope then said:

— The choice is this: you can choose whether to be the murderer or the victim.

At this the ice that had held Nilus rigid, and that alone had allowed him to sustain the presence of the dark Truth, began to melt. He folded and crumpled and hung and slid in his chair as if there were no man left in his clothes and the open "Oh no.o.o.o.o..." that came from him was like the little wind of his life escaping.

His hands went to his face and huge hot tears poured over them and he sobbed and couldn't breathe and couldn't see, until he was a snivelling mess. He was ashamed and he despised himself and he couldn't stand being this wet helpless thing and yet he was. He found a tissue and wiped himself and looked up at the figure, tears still pouring, and his voice came out in a croak over the huge lump in his throat.

— Is... that...? Is... there... nothing... I... can... do? Is... there... no way... out?

He didn't expect there was, and he didn't see why there should be. He had been pierced by the figure's words and he accepted the judgement. What else could he do but cry, and cry out to the one who judged him?

— Please, please, you gotta understand. I just didn't know it mattered that much.

Mattered that much, mattered that much. Nilus's mind collapsed. It became molten and whirling. He heard what he was saying and he knew what it meant. First time knew, first time knew. What do you mean you didn't know it mattered that much?

Mattered that much, oh my God, oh my God, what do I mean I didn't know?

What do I mean I didn't know it mattered that much?

Life, my life, life.

Scenes faces betrayals partings losses kisses treacheries triumphs pride emptiness prizes, all whirled round him in succession.

"Oh God," he wept and cried. There was nothing in him to stop

22

him becoming one huge cry. "Oh God, my life, what do I mean I
didn't know it mattered that much? Life, oh God, abortions, oh hell,
oh Christ, this is terrible, what has been happening, is there any way
out, when will it stop, oh God, is there anything I can do to make this
stop? She killed herself and it was me. Of course it was me. Who else?
Who else? I know it was me. I can't stand it, I can't stand me. Please,
please, is there any way to stop this?"

He was pierced judged acquitted and freed, pierced judged acquitted and freed.

— What can I do? Tell me what I can do.

— Stop.

Nilus stopped.

— You can stop. And you can cry for mercy. And you can have
mercy, for mercy is yours to give and receive. But you couldn't have
it without the truth, for the truth is yours too, to give and receive.

Nilus looked up. He could hear the voice but there was no figure.

— No you can't see me now. Only sometimes in extreme peril or
need. But you will always be able to hear me if you wish, and I will
hear you, because everything is one, little one, and the furthest limits
of the universe are as near as the darkest part of your mind.

The voice stopped. The limp and shattered Nilus Absinthe looked
down at his two palmfuls of tears, the broken waters of his new life
upon earth, and fell asleep to the floor.

— Alan Jackson
Poet

Naomi Brandel

Naomi was born in Scotland in 1940. She lived most of her adult life in southwest Cork, Ireland. She had two daughters there, and worked as a sculptor in a smallholding by the sea.

She moved to England and trained as an art therapist; she now lives and works in Gloucestershire.

The New Dispensation

Two weeks after the event, when someone who had been there came up and shared what a beautiful evening it had been — 'magical', a word many friends used — I watched the old apology rise up impotently in me: "Sorry. Sorry all the limelight was on me." Other people's process can seem tedious when you've managed to change the groove records ago, but hold on, because I want to show you how this one may still play with you, how it splices your wings and holds you back in the race to be first at the wakening. Unless, of course, you're charismatic or crazy. The charismatic character has discarded the crumpled bag of self-apology and that's just why we're so attracted to him or her, because they allow us to reflect their shining. Christ is charismatic.

First I need to tell you how it was. A moth's eye view of a magical night. I called it a New Decade Party which in February 1990 seemed appropriate. But in the end I came clean. If you want to celebrate your birthday with friends you have to be prepared to share your age (which I had never thought to obscure until the shock of fifty.) So it was to be an evening of celebration, a birthday party for my new decade and the newly emerged nineties.

My route to this event had passed through the life changes of the forties: conceiving a baby as my marriage was breaking apart; straight into a new relationship that was finished after five years; giving up the family home, changing countries and moving as a single parent with two children from one short-term furnished let to another: five moves in three years. Not being able to cope, I withdrew more and more and spun tight threads to hold myself together. Finally high fever came burning the strictures away; giving in came, and the relief of letting go into the dark mother of sickness, and beyond that, the choice not to die. Not now.

These were the frail bones. But in between, another current was moving, creating a more resilient flesh. Like the first pale stars in the evening, the darker my life grew the more I found brightening friendships around me. The more I learnt to trust in sharing — instead of brave withdrawal ("I don't want to bother you") — the more I found the juices of life returning in fuller measure. I discovered that whenever I was given kindness I would weep. These tears warmed my heart, plumpened my skeletal body. The bald patches on my head began to sprout new growth. Like the infant, the more I was suckled the bonnier I grew.

For many of us, though the story is different, the path is the same. The forties is often a time of things being taken away. Things that feel as fundamental as the ground under your feet. You cannot believe at these moments that the new will be born, that all this pruning is necessary for vigorous growth to appear. Life crisis hones faith at a time when to have faith seems outright naive.

But to return to the moth fluttering high up in the shadows of the barrel-shaped ceiling of the Big Room, or seeking the light of candles on the sills, the warmth of the log fire at one end... The children (the eldest being twenty-two) had come in earlier to decorate the ledges with snowdrops and primroses and to concoct mulled juices in the kitchen next door. I had been sent off to be given a massage by the editor of this book. Gabriel bathed me in oil and love, left me to sleep and finally gave us all supper in the glow of her kitchen.

The evening, you may have gathered, was set in a large house. It is the home of friends who rent out the Big Room for workshops. That weekend "The Wild Man" workshop was running during the day and I like to think they had been preparing the space for us on many levels as we created new space for them to return to the next day.

The constellation of friends gathered and grew and warmed itself. The room enlivened: cakes and wine and the warmth of friendship, presents piled on the grand piano. I had asked people to bring something to contribute of their own, a poem, a song. The story of St. Bride, whose birthday I share, was sung and bathed us all in its simplicity. A silence as the first brave poet stepped out. The quality of the three poems was as tangible as the Word. Something else was born in that celebratory room — awe, a sense of depths and abundant mystery. Another poet stood and tinted our inner world with the first rainbow colours. Then I knew I could keep silence no longer. I first shared my terror of singing in public. "It would be helpful if I could breathe." But some Prospero filled my lungs and the songs sailed high, curving the ceiling and brought us more manna.

More songs, more cake, more awe. And then Tara did her dance.

Tara is twenty-two, my daughter, a dancer in training. Since she started college four years ago I had never seen her dance anything of her own. This one she had choreographed for my birthday. What I hadn't known was she had written an accompanying poem and learnt a breathing technique so she could dance and speak the music of her poem at the same time.

She knelt tall on the floor, thick red hair, her body lithe in the dark folds of her dress. Her hands began the dance. "To my mother..." When she stood to weave her body, her voice grew in strength fed by deep breaths like the bellows of the Illen pipes. Her dance leapt over the floor, swayed in the shadows, grew mighty in the vaulted ceiling and entered the earth. We followed her, rapt. All the time her voice intoned the words:

To my mother
A strong woman
Tall and steady like a tree
Who feels the movements of the earth
And reaches out her hopes to the sky

To my mother
A trusting woman
Certain and positive like a child
Who steadily believes in the rightness of life
And the lessons that it teaches

To my mother
A creative woman
Intuitive and subtle like a witch
Who paints her visions of what she truly sees
And warms her home with song

To my mother
A wise woman
On this her 50th year
Still being
Mother daughter lover child friend
To us all

Naomi. Here is my present to you
Happy Birthday

My younger daughter confided to me afterwards that she meant at this point to play a piece on her cello for me, but following Tara's dance felt too difficult. It remains my one regret of the evening that she didn't play.

At this point when our hearts were streaming, Barbara produced a huge tray covered with nightlights (fifty of course). She asked me if I would take one, light it and tell us about some happy experience of childhood. And light another to a happy experience in my teens.

27

Another and another, to each of my daughters. She invited everyone else to come up one by one and light a candle to me and speak of how we first met and anything else we might like to share.

As I sat with each friend in the increasing glow of candlelight, laughed at our story together, heard their perceptions of me through my changes, saw through their eyes what knowing me had been for them, the mirroring grew brighter. My neighbour the next day said to me how astonishing it was to hear people talking from their hearts. "You usually only hear people say things like that about someone if they are dying or dead." A sad observation on our society that we only reflect the highest in a person when it's too late.

There was a moment of doubt. Thirty or so sharings takes time and was anyone out there, waiting in the shadows, bored by this pageant? I turned to the friend next to me. "Is it alright?" His smiling assurance, "It's enchanting", was genuine. I stepped back into heart-warmth and joy. Into the dream. The nagual.

What I was learning was all around receiving. If I blocked through embarrassment what was coming towards me, it felt like rejecting a gift. Each time I entered into the cave of light with another I realised the way I could help them create, step through any fear of sharing from their soul, was to open myself to them. This allowed the dance, let the energy move between us. I learnt that receiving is just another form of giving. The duality becomes one.

After the last sharing, when all the candles were flickering, after I blew them out, Jehanne, Rob and Will, our local troubadours, played their music. Jehanne's songs are her personal journey, a distillation of her pain, her happiness, her love. As she grows, her songs grow in depth and beauty. They are a remembering not only of our origins but of our original promise. These, her latest work, carried us mellow and joy-filled into the last part of the night.

Looking at my story from thirty-six to fifty, I can see and experience it as a rite of passage. Marion Woodman in *The Pregnant Virgin* says, "Many people in our culture are attempting to suffer these transformations alone, without any ritual container and without any group to support the influx of transcendent power. Like Eliot's Magi they experience the birth as 'hard and bitter agony... like Death, our death'. They are 'no longer at ease here, in the old dispensation. With an alien people clutching their gods'."

That night I found my ritual container and my group. I 'wafted in the God' with them, was given the gift of carrying through the vehicle of my being this new dispensation which included us all.

In the weeks that followed, as the shining in me still continues and through the enormous gratitude I feel for what I've been given, I know my vane has changed direction, the old apology has lost its grip. In *Change of Life* Ann Mankowitz talks of the final stage of a rite of passage as a "ceremony of rebirth and renewal — the return of a changed being into society and the world". The evening has taken me through some final stage of a transformation begun unconsciously fourteen years ago. Parents talk about the changes in childhood — it's only a phase — other phases will follow. But with a little help from my friends this one is completed.

The chorus of one of Jehanne's songs, which we all joined in, had the last word that evening.

Straight down the middle
And out the other side
Straight down the middle
And out the other side!

— Naomi Brandel
Sculptor and Painting Therapist

Jehanne Mehta

Jehanne Mehta writes and sings. She is married, has three grown-up children and lives in Gloucestershire.

Straight Down the Middle

(Song)

The sun was going down behind a bank of crimson mist;
We were open and exposed along the empty road at dusk.
The sound we made was tiny, but the echoes won't stop rolling;
The world was shifting focus and the poles were in reverse.
We have lit the blue touch paper and we can't escape the blaze;
And you said, "Straight down the middle and out the other side,
Straight down the middle and out the other side."

They were watching us intently in the sky and in the stones;
They had weighed up all the anguish but the choice had to be ours.
All we did was touch hands, but the current won't stop flowing;
The contact was established then and love was on the move.
We have lit the blue touch paper and we can't escape the blaze;
And you said, "Straight down the middle and out the other side,
Straight down the middle and out the other side."

We may choose to deny it, we may turn the other way,
Pretend it never happened, it was just a missing day;
But the stones have not forgotten and the earth still keeps on humming:
It took so long to get here and it lasted but three days;
And the time too short to understand the meaning of this place,
And the time too soon to understand how deep the story is;
And you said, "Straight down the middle and out the other side,
Straight down the middle and out the other side."

But it is night still on the road
And I am reaching to your heart,
And there are fears that come between
With some intent to undermine;
But the sunrise won't be long
And we are free to take it on,
And it's still, "Straight down the middle and out the other side,
Straight down the middle and out the other side."

— Jehanne Mehta

31

Francis Martineau

Francis Martineau spent his first twenty-five years in Scotland, moving to New York for his Ph.D at Columbia, and then on to the University of Toronto, where he taught theatre for sixteen years.

As well as teaching classes in directing, stage theory and improvisation, he created a new drama department and published articles on the contemporary theatre scene.

In 1982 he resigned from the University and moved to California, where he has been engaged in his own private practice. He works with individuals and groups, applying his knowledge of theatre to the healing arts, and encouraging people to contact their true creative source.

In 1989 he wrote and directed a cycle of four plays, *Rites: Passage to Self,* in which the players enacted their own process of self-discovery, and he has recently completed a book about his own approaches to healing, entitled *The Sensitive Vein.*

Mother Turns

I was eighteen when she died and innocence demanded she be cast, as she had always been, in a fiery blaze of perfection. When she was alive, its brightness hurt my eyes, its heat scorched my heart. I never could endure the burning. She was dead now, so I turned and ran. I ran and kept running, not knowing the reason why.

Several years later, on the other side, her opposite rose to meet me. She welcomed me with cool brilliant detachment and shuttered heart, safe harbour from the passion I could not own. She took me in and protected me, until my heart began to die. I was still dying when she left me, untouched, untouchable, unaware of the consequences of my own precipitous flight.

She had been eighteen years alive and eighteen years dead when, one afternoon, I was touched again. I was touched and so could begin to return. Inch by inch I crawled back along the path I had fled so blindly, not into the perfection now, but into the longing, the loss and the pain. Into the dawning awareness that, in all her comings and goings, in all her heroic beauty, she had never, as human being, made herself known to me. I cried out as I crawled: "Who are you, woman? Who are you? Tell me who you are."

Fresh memory echoed back at me, information unknown. Confused substance of flesh and blood, reverberation of the real, innocence gasping for air. Then, as reward for my quest, I found her again, found her in another voice, another body, another age. I did not know it was she. When she was in disguise and all I could feel were the warmth of her open arms and a faint memory in the loving of her eyes. I re-entered the spell of enchantment, accepting again the fiery perfection that I could not withstand before. For a time I was at rest, couched in disguise, my crying for knowledge submerged.

Then subtly, beneath the skein of enchantment, she stirred, dancing sinister in the space between. Little by little she made herself known to me and the wrestle in earnest began. Innocence and perfection finally thrown and chaos revealed. Love and cruelty criss-crossing in a wild frenzy of upheaval, joining forces so that the terrible alchemy could be revealed. I cried out again as I wrestled, now in a voice of terror and rage: "You are crazy, I see that now. I was plaything for a lunatic that lies in you. But that is not all. That is only a blind for what I cannot see. I still do not know who you are. Unless I know who you are, I will never be free."

For a long time we wrestled together, closely locked, anger and exhilaration pulsing in waves. Then, one morning in the dawn's light, I saw her true. The vision was bright, but it did not burn. The final layer, a mere shadow. A woman in dire need, gasping for breath, barely able to express, now she had been exposed, the extent of her weakness and her pain. Behind the power and fearlessness, a fragility crumbling to dust, unbelievable, unbearable to behold. Behind the craziness, my own sensitivity, shattered beyond compare.

Since then, I catch glimpses only, curtains spontaneously raised to reveal a landscape completely unknown. So unknown, so washed clean, so unlike the experience of my life so far that it takes my breath away. I am not there yet. I cannot move. I can only take in the stretch of landscape and imagine my first faltering steps outside. Imagine one step, then another and another, before looking up at an unfamiliar woman standing there. We are face to face and my mother is not dancing in the space between. Her reckless theatre no longer intervenes. I see details for the first time, clear focus, no tangles of seduction, showing me the true line. A hint of possibility only, then she is gone. The landscape fades. The rooms of my past enclose me again and the curtains fall.

Imprints are deep, transitions slow. Cells rearrange themselves with infinite patience as I rage and storm. Quick flickers of lightning confirm the changes as they enter in. With every flash my mother turns, spiralling downwards from her throne of power. The seat is empty. I am quiet now. And still. No words can fill the void, shape the next unknown. No steps be prelude to the dance that will move me when the curtains rise for the last time and there is no return.

— Francis Martineau
Writer and Drama Therapist

Diana Durham

Diana Durham has worked in administration, journalism, marketing and independent television production. She has been associated with the Emissary Foundation International since she was 18, and has run many public meetings and workshops on practical spirituality and group process.

Since 1965 she has been writing poetry. In 1987 she won the Plas Glyn-Y-Weddw Short Story Competition, and has completed her first novel. She has published two books of poetry, *Fire Path* and *Sea of Glass*. Some of her poems are being set to music by composer Rosemary Duxbury.

Fire

I was eighteen. I was staying in a spiritually-based community in the Caribou region of British Columbia. Everything was new to me: the land, the people, their philosophy. I had come to visit my aunt and uncle, and had no idea that they lived communally. I was worried that I would be brainwashed by the eighty or so residents of this strange place.

Everyone worked there, on the cattle ranch, in the kitchen, cleaning the various communal buildings: meeting room, dining room, offices, lounges. So in the end, as there wasn't much else to do, I joined in, but reluctantly — this wasn't my idea of a holiday!

Everyone was amazingly kind and friendly to me, but at the same time, I could tell that there was no emotional investment in me, in what I did, in 'winning me over', in whether I liked what was going on or not. If I wanted to join in, that was fine; if I didn't, that was also fine. This impressed me.

Eventually, after about five weeks of my stay there, I was won over. I still didn't understand what it was all about — they spoke about 'being in the moment', 'it's not what you do that's important, but who you are'. They told me not to try to understand it with my mind. All I really knew was that there was something about these people that I liked, something that rang deeply true; they were vibrant, genuine, more alive than most people I had met before.

And in this atmosphere, without really realising it, I had begun to open up, to shed some of my inhibitions and teenage sadnesses; I was expressing a fuller current of joy and loveliness. And one evening, at yet another little social gathering in someone's small log cabin home, I was drinking tea, talking and laughing with everyone else, when something began to happen. I suddenly felt a power starting to build inside; a hugely powerful flow was welling up, rising up, like a great golden sun. I knew it was love, I knew it was truth, it was who I was, who everyone really was. It was the fire. I was so strong, so radiant.

I started to wonder if anyone could see what was happening, if I was transfigured in some way. I said something about a power building up inside me, and a friend said: "Don't worry, you'll be able to handle it when you go home." And I realised she didn't really understand what was happening. And then the power, the gold, subsided. It hadn't lasted very long. But I knew that it was what all the religions and mystery traditions were talking about, that it was the source of us, and it was enough.

— Diana Durham
Poet

Brian Oosthuysen

Brian was born in Port Elizabeth in South Africa on 3rd April 1938. He left South Africa at the height of the Sharpville Crisis in 1961, intent on becoming a priest. He studied at Kings College, London, with Desmond Tutu (as a young curate) but a marriage break-up thwarted his plans.

He is now happily married to Carole and lives in Stroud. They have four children.

'I accepted an invitation to a dinner'

It is often noticeable how ordinary are the events which drastically and, in many cases, irrevocably redirect one's life.

When I look back now, at 53, to the events which changed a naive, unthinking young man of 17 or 18, it was the comparatively minor acts which were pivotal. I have always believed that the story of the conversion of Saul on the Damascus road was no sudden, dramatic event. Of course, there was the occasion of the vision and the subsequent events which changed this fanatical persecutor of Christianity into one of the great leaders of the Christian church in the first century, but I am convinced that, when he set out on that fateful day, he was already a troubled man, an uncertain man, a man hiding his fear — as so many of us do — by an apparently strong, unyielding exterior, a fear possibly re-enforced by many small incidents.

I was, in the 1950's (in South Africa), a typical 'white' South African youth. I believed, if I ever thought about it at all, that the system of Apartheid, which I now regard as an unmitigated evil, was part of the Natural scheme of things. Accepting my privileged status without question, I pursued my enjoyment of that status with a mind untrammelled by doubt or uncertainty.

Beach, sun, sand and girls in Durban, however, was clearly not enough. There must have been that 'still, small voice of God' calling patiently, unheard in the conscious state but bubbling up occasionally from the depths of the unconscious. And yet, the beginning of change was commonplace. I accepted an invitation to a dinner given by St. Paul's Church in Durban as part of its mission endeavours.

I remember nothing of the meal except meeting Jimmy Draper, the curate, who by a quiet word, a friendly smile and a total acceptance of this rather gauche young man, became the way in which God finally called to me.

Suddenly — over the next days and weeks, and without warning — questions came unbidden into my mind. Urgent questions, demanding of an answer I couldn't give with any satisfaction without changing my lifestyle, my priorities and my profoundest beliefs and suppositions, shallow though they might have been, and accepting a deep belief in the God of Love. C.S. Lewis says in his autobiography that when he finally accepted a belief in God, he crossed the divide kicking and screaming, possibly the most reluctant convert in England. I knew exactly what he meant, except that mine was no reluctant conversion, but a change that finally became inevitable.

There was a dramatic occurrence which took place about this time, an occurrence in which, however, I played a minor part and yet which, in a subtle way, forwarded my change of heart, soul and mind and which, I felt, fitted into the whole pattern of conversion which was hardening — if one could use such a word — into the belief I now profess.

On my way to a church meeting at a new friend's house, I witnessed a policeman kicking a black thief to death, after disarming him. An admiring group of whites encircled the two of them, the black man on the ground grunting in pain as the heavy-booted policeman kicked him remorselessly into a painful death.

Two things happened to me as I watched. The first was an overwhelming shame at not protesting at this grossly violent attack, a shame I would not have felt before my change of heart. And secondly, a feeling, a gnawing resolve, that — in this sad, troubled and violent country of my birth, change, strong, deep, permanent change was needed in the hearts of oppressed and oppressors alike, and that the change had to begin in me first. I am now a pacifist. After that the change was complete. In my own small way, I echoed Saul on my own Damascus road.

— Brian Oosthuysen
Schoolteacher and Administrator

Alice Friend

Alice Friend was born in 1948 and brought up in Vancouver, British Columbia. She moved to England in 1973, and there developed her mediumistic talents.

She has worked with colour for many years, and created Rainbow healing sweaters that have helped heal and balance many people.

She trained in counselling and shamanistic Medicine Wheel work.

Now she lives with her second husband, son and step-son, working with a group in Stroud trying to create a sustainable village.

My Inner Guide

There have been many profound experiences in my life, but I would like to share the one that has had the greatest effect on the evolution of my soul. What comes to mind at the moment is the saying, **Seek ye first the kingdom of heaven and all else will be given unto you.** In my case, this has most definitely been so!

I first came into contact consciously with my inner guide, Golden Flame, at a meditation at the White Eagle Lodge. I felt this presence beside me of enormous love and an actual physical warmth. I got a quick 'flash' of an Egyptian priest, but as I was to learn very quickly, his form or definition was not what I was to focus on. Instead it was the receiving of enormous unconditional love and a great deal of inner wisdom and teachings.

I was told by a palmist when I was twenty that I was a medium. Many times after that I was also told by other people who felt they saw a destiny around me. I must admit that I had been receiving songs since I was 16 and I never knew quite what I had written till the filled paper was in front of me and I had to learn it! So the so-called mediumship started with my song writing when I was a teenager. It wasn't for many years, however, that this gift would become consciously manifest, and through some courtship and trial and error at that!

After my initial experience of this warm and loving presence with me, it became a common experience, and one which felt extremely secure and pleasant. Slowly I started to know that I could choose to converse with this being if I became pure from any negative thoughts or emotions. I knew that a very deep friend was with me, one who loved me beyond any experience of love I had ever encountered before. In fact, it made human love and relationship seem quite blind and ignorant. When I looked at and thought about the world around me and the so-called communication of people, I fell into quite a depression for a while because I realized that we were supposed to love each other as God loves us, and that we have been given no example in our lives to do this, except maybe Jesus and the other great and mature teachers, but not society or our parents!

Through time and trial, and also with the help of Ruth White and Gildas, as well as the White Eagle Lodge, I started more and more to communicate with and to accept this Inner Guide. When I left my husband and bought a cottage in the Slad Valley, I was suddenly pushed into a position where I was a single Mum and had to cope more on my own. I am a semi-hermit and love my times alone, so I started using these times to get closer to my guide Golden Flame. In one meditation with him he actually asked me to 'marry' him, and I laughed and said maybe we could try it out first by living together!

Well, as fate had it, in a wonderfully enlightening workshop with Ruth White at this time, she took us all on an inner journey, and there was Golden Flame to tell me that I was on the threshold of my destiny. It was a very real experience and he asked me again to commit to him. I said I would, knowing that it would be a big step, and not knowing what was in store from that commitment.

He asked to have made a white gold ring to place on the middle finger of my left hand, next to my now empty wedding ring finger, which he said would have a ring on it when the right time came and we would all be together. I had this white gold ring made with the mantra *Om Namah Shivaya* engraved on it, which means, "may the highest of God's will be done".

In a ceremony and ritual that I put time aside for, I went through a most profound inner marriage to my guide, and from that time onwards my life has been within the commitment of that moment. In 'marrying' Golden Flame, I was told by him that he would always look after me. I must say that, over the years, he has proved to do just that, and much, much more.

I started quite professionally channelling him. At first to willing friends who sought advice and healing, and then to clients who started to hear of the wisdom of Golden Flame. During this time I was also getting inner teachings and answers to questions that I took to him about many things. His answers were always based on enormous love and acceptance and also the complete honouring of my free will to choose whether or not to take the advice he suggested. It was not only advice — I was also receiving deep and lovely teachings about my own soul and the love of God. These teachings were simple and pure and, from the experience of them, proved always to be right, as long as my channelling was disciplined enough not to have any of my own emotions or lower ego fears in the way.

The actual experience of the commitment was the force behind the whole thing. For now I know that commitment is a real spiritual discipline, and creates its own life that helps enormously the strength of what the commitment is based upon. The commitment was not just to a guide called Golden Flame; it was to my God-Self within, and it still is, no matter what the name is, or the form it takes. This is the commitment, in my experience, to the higher and purer state of my consciousness, without the let down and pulling away from that by the ego and personality. I recognize Truth from that pure state of simple and accepting Divine Love.

These things are often very hard to put into words or explanations, but I can say that one day of inner marriage has changed my life, my thoughts, my aspirations, my values and my life as much as anything has done. I have always been drawn to loving teachings, and find the teachings of White Eagle so beautiful and pure and 'home' for me as much as any. My parents were always sharing their experience of meditation, and books and discussions were always around in the family atmosphere that I was brought up in.

This experience of the inner marriage, though, was one that was my own experience and came directly from inner guidance and this inner presence of my Divine nature. This presence continues. I have published nine newsletters based on Golden Flame's teachings and many, many people have come to ask questions. It has also taken me to Brussels twice and I have given many workshops around the country to help others discover and hear their inner guide.

It is an experience that is ongoing. Like any marriage, it has its ups and downs, mostly based on my fears and lack of faith. My children have benefited from this commitment of mine because I was also told by Golden Flame that they were to be a priority and that they were my greatest ongoing lessons in everyday life. I am sure that everyone who has children would say the same! They have grown up knowing their mother is married to a spiritual guide! However, Golden Flame's words were correct as usual, and I do indeed have a ring on my wedding ring finger now and am united in love with a wonderful and supportive man.

The beauty of the inner guide is not one of form or image — it is one of the presence of Divine Love, and a catalyst to God, in fact, an ambassador of God. This ambassador, in my experience, is the purest part of myself. My personality and conditioning always get in the way of that purest part, and over the years, with the constant living with this inner guidance, I have found very slowly all other aspects of my life merge with that greater one. My values and thoughts and every day life have changed enormously since that commitment, and it is from that commitment that my greatest steps forward are taken — it gives me enormous inner and outer strength that I did not have before.

So, the greatest breakthrough and experience of my life was that commitment, that marriage to my God-Self. It did take the appearance of an inner guide separate from myself, but somewhere behind all that there is a great joke — for there is no separation, and I am learning, slowly, the Oneness of all life from this Oneness within myself.

— Alice Friend
Medium

Roger Finnegan

Roger Finnegan was born in Manchester in 1953. He is the father of two children, and works as a landscape gardener in the West Midlands.

"Someone's here beside us"

Through the aberration,
the archetype becomes apparent
— Goethe

The clinic's long approach had that timeless familiarity associated with the advent of the inevitable — not so much the recognition of a physical location, more the growing awareness that all life's roads had been leading to this place, everything was being funnelled down this holly-lined lane to a half-expected who knows what. I sat fragmented in the passenger seat, oscillating between hopeful anticipation and the dismissive sneer of rejection. Part of me had had enough and didn't mind if this was really the end of the road. Through circumstances of my own making and others out of my control, I found myself homeless, my family estranged, penniless on the doorstep of a charitable institution looking for some answers to the whims of outrageous fortune, if only to die laughing at the irony.

It soon became clear that it would be a long haul and the usual three to six week visit would not apply in my case. I was installed in a room and a program of therapies and slowly found my way around the life of the place.

The longer term patients, often peers of those in like plight, would tend to congregate in the smoke room, aside from the main lounge. It was a bit of a den, a hangout confessional for fears and petty conspiracies to find voice and disperse on voile wings with the smoke and quiet prayers breathed in there. As time passed and the blurred dance of admissions and departures sent the treated back to loved ones, to new lives, or to die, there remained a group of three regular faces (questionably) all male between twenty-eight and thirty-five, some of Irish ancestry and prone to despair.

The rural setting of the clinic gave it the dual role of sanctuary and confinement. Dermot, Lee and I formed a temporary social reference for each other and served as an extra-therapeutic counselling service, having had many common experiences outside the medical staff's field of expertise or direct knowledge. This had its negative side also as there was ample scope for reinforcing self deceptions and creating an 'us and them' mentality. Truth will out in the end and we eventually tired of each other's excuses and cannibal spirals to nowhere. Nonetheless, for a short time the rib and jaw aching round of manic humour was refreshing, if not life saving.

Brisk walks on the lanes and wooded slopes had been a regular event since early on in our unholy alliance, and we would stomp off our frustrations or bark them out as caricatures while beating the dead grass and thistle heads with sticks as though they were the enemy that laid siege upon our fragile empire. We usually returned spent and nervously furtive like the remnant of a ragged army in occupied territory.

As Advent of that year drew in for each of us, and our personal sense of loss and loneliness, our walks in the wild wood became less frantic. It was as if the season asked a more reverent passing, asked of us a stillness and yet acute attention. Lee had become increasingly withdrawn and cynical, Dermot perpetually didn't know anything anymore, and I just muttered positive observations out of habit while falling apart inside. Separation from the kids at this time of year was the hardest test of my life.

We strung out in the plantations with our own preoccupations and, at last, recognizable identities. Lee was dark and brooding as the pines, fierce and bright when ignited. Dermot was airy but brittle like lime wood, and I guess I was the elm laid low by disease but still alright for hedging.

There was a hushed mood inside these woods like a frosted indrawn breath, held but tingling with anticipation, alive with possibilities. A deer or pheasant would suddenly break cover as if the tension was too much to bear and exposed flight was preferable to anxious hiding. Each time the silence settled more intense, condensed until it was almost as tangible as the timber, or rather allowed the timber to emerge from this body of stillness. Dermot and I exchanged quizzical glances, sensing simultaneously a question that we had no words to formulate other than with the eloquence of the body stances and facial expressions that confirmed that we were aware of something but could not name it.

Eventually, we emerged from beneath the shaded eaves into golden winter sunlight as it slanted across the vaporous veils that fringed the woods. Dermot and I were some way in front and were stopped in our tracks as inner experience and outer symbol merged into a unity. The mists parted in a majestically simple gesture and left the naked branches turned to gold. Dermot finally voiced what was by now obvious to us both: "Someone's here beside us."

I could only nod and grin a quiet mirth's agreement, not wanting to mar the blessed moment with clumsy words, though an explanation, as if one were needed, spoke through me stating factually that 'this is how the Christ appears'. Wave on wave of warm security bathed through and over all my being. A calm, exquisite, peaceful power, self-evident, with nothing to prove, bridged myself to all things and they to me and still the waves washed on deeper, ever deeper, through very blood and bone. These waves seemed to emanate from a figure that somehow was static and yet in motion at one and the same time. A beautiful being, neither male nor female but more, so much more, than the best of both, distinct and yet indistinguishable from everything. Ultimate reality, total perception, words cease to explain or else turn into a zealot's gibbering.

Lee came up to us completely oblivious of any such occurrence and was scathing in his dismissal. Maybe his own unrecognized light sparked the whole event. But that's all speculation. Until recently I had thought we had been just fortunate witnesses to a remarkable gift in difficult times, that we were given a one-off treasure to keep as consolation.

It has since turned up in various conversations and would appear to be an increasingly common experience, and in recalling the events of that time I find that I reconnect with something essential, not in a covetous static way, but as in a conversation, ongoing and developing with each re-exploration of themes related.

The idea of a future ancestry is the only way that I can encompass the gist of it. All I know is that any tyrant can come before those parting veils and find a brother with the strength to understand, and find guidance on the way of transformation.

— Roger Finnegan
Gardener

Charles Lawrie

I grew up in North Wales, after my twin sister and I were carried South from 'Auld Reekie' in late 1947, aged six weeks.

Now I'm back there again, on the Celtic West, as I turn my pen to articles, poems etc. I am a correspondent for *Novalis*.

I believe in the integrity of humanity; we shall prevail, because we are created to create, out of freedom and love.

Ring me at 0766 513747. Your friend, Charles Lawrie.

A Testimony

Walking across George IV Bridge Street, as my beloved Grandmother lay dying in the autumn city of Edinburgh, I did not know my feet were on a path.

Like many, I had passed through the wilderness of adolescence chiefly with the help of the spirit of Beethoven. His last piano sonatas, his late string quartets seemed to console all the loneliness of psychic isolation. He was my brother — a great all-human affirmative transmuter of suffering into the dove-like flutterings of the Holy Spirit.

As my Grandmother lay, propped in her bed, under the sheltering embrace of the Pentland hills — *I will lift up mine eyes unto the hills, from whence cometh my help* — I would place the slow movement of Mozart's *Sinfonia Concertante* upon the gramophone, and we would pass into the wordless empathy of which that music is so wonderful an expression. Later, I learned that Mozart had composed it following, perhaps literally, the death of his own mother. Here were the Oistrakhs, father and son, singing together, and here were my Grandmother and I, celebrating the song of eternal friendship.

My feet took me on. The windows of Alexander Grant, Bookseller, Antiquarian and Second Hand, came by. I stopped, and looked in.

At the age of 16 I had awoken to the striving for knowledge which school did not provide. I had sought amid all the literature which I and friends could find for the knowing which would satisfy this striving. Yet still I sought, near nineteen, like one in the desert, for the unknown wellspring of life.

Kneeling one day at school to repeat the Lord's Prayer in the privacy of my room, I had risen and thrown off formal religion, the credal Christianity of my upbringing, in a single decision. This was folly. There was no God.

The pain of this awareness, or lack of it, drove me on. Through poetry, literature, mysticism. I found psychology — J.C. Flügel's wonderful account of its first hundred years, of Freud and Adler and Jung, which opened the observation of psychic facts. This had led to philosophy. Bertrand Russell pointed to Augustine, and via Augustine, who could not doubt his doubting, to Descartes. In Descartes' *Meditations* I found the indubitable observation of the act of doubting, the self-certifying phenomenon of consciousness conscious of itself. Though the Frenchman moved in his presentation

51

from phenomenology to rationalism, nevertheless: here was one principle on which true knowing could reside: the act, the fact, of self-knowing.

Now I began to attend with new ears to the speech of spiritual scriptures. In the Bhagavad-Gita I sensed the same spiritual voice, though more remote, which seemed to resound in the Gospel of John. While in the first Yoga Sutra of Patanjali: *"yoga citta vritti nirodha"* (rendered by Ernest Wood c. "Yoga is control of the fluctuations of the mind") and in the exercise of 'one-pointed' *samadhi*, I found the same seed-essence of concentration upon one's mental activity more formally acknowledged by Descartes, and observed by Krishnamurti in attending to the unconditioned act of attention — freedom from, but also, for the known. Gradually I began to discern the essence of Christianity — no longer appearing as a product of belief within the mind, but approaching spiritually as a real entity in the world. I sought the world.

Another Frenchman came towards me: Pierre Teilhard de Chardin, Jesuit and Paleontologist, whose profound love of the Earth and spiritual exercises led him to a perspective of the whole of world-evolution centring in Christ and culminating in the Pauline vision **"En pasi panta Theos"**, 1 Cor. v. 28: "That God may be all in all". In some measure, he was aware of the Cosmic Christ of the Apocalypse: "I am Alpha and Omega, the beginning and the ending". He found the fire at the foundation of world-creation, and saw creation returning, freely, into that state of fire, renewed. World-evolution could become a Bhagavad-Gita, a mutual song of the Lord.

Here was another valid principle, a world-evolutionary perspective, to place beside the self-perception of the questioning being (Descartes). Here was the principle of world-metamorphosis and world-integration through and in Christ.

To me, at that time, it seemed that these two principles stood at the forefront of contemporary human knowing. No principle, that I knew of, exceeded them in certainty or scope. Surely they should be united?

But who had done this? I knew of no-one. So, I thought to myself: you must do it yourself. You must try to bring these two principles — the principle of human self-knowing, and of world-Christification — together, like the twin pillars of a doorway. But who knows what may unfold the other side?

I opened the door of Alexander Grant's and walked in. The spacious scene, the scent of leather, joined with the fishbowl silence of men browsing. In the back-room, up a step-ladder, my eye fell upon the azure spine of a hardback, its title: *The Faithful Thinker*. It was 1966. The jacket spoke of Rudolf Steiner: "The Austrian philosopher has a unique place as a visionary among scientists and a scientist among visionaries... this book forms an admirable introduction to one of the most comprehensive minds of modern times". This was interesting — but the words that leapt at me formed the title of a chapter by Alfred Heidenreich, Ph.D.: "The Re-Discovery of the Cosmic Christ". I bought the book, and went out.

In Heidenreich's account, I found the two principles of human cognition and world-evolution uniting in Rudolf Steiner's spiritual-scientific recognition of the stages of the development of Jesus Christ. I had to say to myself, in some surprise, of Rudolf Steiner: "Here is someone who already, fifty years before my time, has proceeded far further upon this path than I have."

But still I wanted to find the essence of this path for myself. And so I did, in a room on Stanford Avenue in Brighton, when, at the age of 21, I grasped for myself the true content of a characterization in Rudolf Steiner's doctoral dissertation "Truth and Science". This passage mediates the self-comprehension of the eternal human spirit in its act of cognition — free of the body, unconditional, self-clear and alight. For Rudolf Steiner (whatever else may be taken from him), *is* the discoverer of the category of cognition, of the cognition of cognition. This is the foundation of science, and it is the category of the free human spirit, which Beethoven voiced, and for which Mozart prepared. It is the realm of the Virgin Birth, the Immaculate Conception, the act of the self-conception of the Human Spirit — and I will leave it in your hands now, dear reader, to test once more, like me, if this is true:

> *Both outer and inner perceptions, as well as its own presence are given immediately to the "I", which is the 'centre of consciousness'. The I feels a need to discover more in the given than is immediately contained in it. In contrast to the given world, a second world — the world of thinking — rises up within the I and the I unites the two in that, through its own free decision, it realizes what we have defined as the idea of cognition. Herein lies a fundamental distinction between the way in which, in the object of human consciousness itself, concept and the immediately-given unite to form full reality, and the way in which this manifests in all other contents of the world. With every other part of the world-picture, we must conceive that the union is the original condition, necessary from beforehand, and that only at the outset of knowing for knowing itself an artificial separation occurs, which is then however overcome, cancelled out, through final knowing, in accordance with the original essence of the object known. But with human consciousness, it is different. Here the*

uniting only eventuates, when it is actively brought about by this consciousness itself. With every other object the separation has no significance for the object but only for the process of knowing. The union is here primary, and the separation derivative. The act of knowing simply occasions the separation, since it cannot in its own way arrive at the possession of the union, unless there is previous separation. Concept and immediately given reality of consciousness, however, are originally separated; their uniting is derivative, and hence the nature of consciousness is constituted in the way we have described. Just because, in consciousness, idea and given content are necessarily separated, total reality divides itself for consciousness into these two parts; and just because consciousness can bring about the unity of the two aforesaid elements only through its own activity, so it can attain to full Reality only through performing the act of cognition. All other categories (Ideas), whether or not they are grasped in cognition, are necessarily united with their corresponding forms of the given. But the idea of knowing can be united with its corresponding given only by the activity of consciousness. Consciousness as a reality exists only if it produces itself.

from Chapter VI of Rudolf Steiner's "Truth and Science"

— Charles Lawrie
Poet and Editor

Bottom Line

Carole Bruce

Carole Bruce is a photographer. She lives in the Slad Valley in Gloucestershire and has four gorgeous grown-up children.

Do You Want to Live?

I sat in the bath, rubbing myself with honey-scented jelly, a Christmas present from my eldest son. It was New Year's Eve. Then I felt it: a hard lump at the top of my left breast. My immediate reaction was, "Oh yes, Cancer now," — no real surprise — my path had been pretty rocky for several years and there was a ghastly inevitability about this latest happening.

The next few weeks were a mass of tests, examinations, hopes, tears, an operation and finally the confirmation that the lump was indeed Cancer. It was all rather unreal. I felt as though I was acting in a film and the director would soon call "Cut". Small incidents stood out; watching men planting trees on a busy traffic island and wondering about their chances of living to achieve their full stature. A very old lady crossing the road in front of my car carrying a bag with 'Peace' written right across it. The love and support of friends and family was firm but I was incredibly alone.

Or was I? Shortly after I started my course of daily radiotherapy, I was sitting on a bus when I heard a clear voice "Do you want to live?" I actually turned around; no one was there but the voice was insistent, "Do you want to live?" "Yes," I said. "Why?" came the voice. I gave answers, my children, friends, my vision. True answers... but they sounded strangely hollow. During the next months the voice became a regular companion, like a visiting Zen Master. It usually came at the most mundane times, not when I was meditating or praying, more likely when I was peeling potatoes or doing an assignment for work.

Four months later I was declared clear by the doctors and I stopped visiting the hospital hardware. My life had changed profoundly — new job, new relationships, new me, I felt. Yet, was I changing enough to prevent myself developing Cancer again? Did I really want to live at the deepest level, knowing that life is a great lesson with a stern teacher? The voice continued and at Easter, over a year after I had received my all clear, I fell into a trough of misery. I thought that if I could get the right answer for my questioner, I would be reprieved. And I couldn't get the right answer to this endless riddle.

Depressed and shaky, my companion and I set off for a short holiday in a remote part of North Wales. The first morning of our stay I set off for a walk over the Traeth — the Great Sands — silence, space, the sea to my left, the peak of Snowdon to my right. Suddenly, everything changed. I became the sea, the sand, the mountains, the sky.

The gulls and I were one, there was no separation anywhere, no questions, no answers... just God within and without, melting into a seamless oneness. How long this experience continued for, I have no idea.

I slowly returned to the cottage, the moment had passed, but I knew I would never need the question again. My answers had passed from my head to my heart and were unspeakable. There was no right or wrong about them. The question had scoured deep into my soul to cleanse and reclaim it. I honoured the mystery and gave thanks for the supreme grace bestowed upon me.

— Carole Bruce
Photographer

David Whyte

Born in Yorkshire in 1955 and educated in England and Wales, he lived for a number of years in South America, where he worked as a Naturalist Guide in the Galapagos Islands and led natural history expeditions in the Andes.

After travels in Asia and a few years directing educational programs, including two years in Oxford, he and his wife and son live in Washington state in the U.S.

He is engaged full-time as a poet, reading and lecturing across the U.S. and his native British Isles.

The Opening of Eyes

After R. S. Thomas

That day I saw beneath dark clouds
the passing light over the water
and I heard the voice of the world speak out,
I knew then, as I had before
life is no passing memory of what has been
nor the remaining pages in a great book
waiting to be read.

It is the opening of eyes long closed.
It is the vision of far off things
seen for the silence they hold.
It is the heart after years
of secret conversing
speaking out loud in the clear air.

It is Moses in the desert
fallen to his knees before the lit bush.
It is the man throwing away his shoes
as if to enter heaven
and finding himself astonished
opened at last
fallen in love with solid ground.

— David Whyte
Songs for Coming Home, 1989,
reprinted by kind permission of
Many Rivers Press, Langley WA, USA

Chloë Goodchild

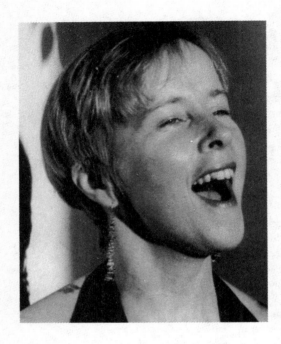

Chloë Goodchild is a singer, a voice teacher, and mother of Rebecca. Sound, sensuality and silence are at the heart of her life and work.

She has produced two albums, *Inner Heat* and *The Voice Inside Her*, which are innovative in bridging Eastern and Western vocal styles. Her book *The Naked Voice* was published by Rider in 1993.

My Body Is The Wind

The call to Non-Separation

'Fill me with your breath, I live on it
I'm your reed, your reed.'

— Rumi

What is this body? And who inhabits it? From where does this breath originate? What is this cycle of life and death, this riddle of mortality, which each person attempts to solve, according to his/her nature? These questions have pursued me throughout my life. For as long as I can remember, I have been aware of 'the Presence'. That is to say, a reality which exists through and beyond the boundaries of my normal senses. A silent reality which dissolves all feelings of separateness, and connects me with this present moment. It can be an electrifying experience, which suddenly stops me in the midst of conversation, when walking down the street, lying in the bath, playing with my daughter, or lifting a glass to my lips.

Of course, it can arise out of more emotionally-heightened situations — when singing, making love, walking through a wood, entering a sacred building, or reading mystical poetry. At such times, I am aware of myself — flesh and blood, heart and mind — as a being abundant with aliveness, fully focused, and inwardly still. It is as if an 'inner observer', or higher intelligence, surfaces out of my usual unconscious activity, expands my awareness, sharpens the listening ear and enables me to witness my everyday reactions with a benign indifference. This all-accepting 'observer within' bridges my ordinary self, with The Self, Brahman, the One-in-all-Things.

This graceful Presence has been a blessed incursion in my life. Yet, until recently, my body/mind has, for the most part, presented me with the irreconcilable 'problem' of the duality of my existence. In other words, there seemed to be no lasting fusion between my physical nature and my spirituality. I was a divided self, a bundle of 'either-ors' drawn in one direction by my attachment to the desires of this world — relationship, cultural activities, creative ambition, food, etc. — and in the other, by my attachment to emptiness, silence and aloneness.

A few years ago, the illusion of this separation between body, mind and spirit, came to an end. One of the events contributing to this was a visit to Northern India. I was staying in Benares, Shiva's homeland, the 'City of Lights', the sacred crematorium ground of India. I found myself standing on the River Ganges, gazing upon six funeral pyres by the water's edge. All around me moved a seething chaos of humanity, old and young, beggars, sadhus, priests, lepers, children playing with kites, thousands of bodies at different stages of living and dying. In the midst of this moved an endless procession of dead corpses, shrouded with coloured cloths, and carried upon stretchers to their final destination — the open fire.

My eyes remained magnetized upon this emotionless death ritual for hours. As time passed, and I watched the disintegration of body after body, from sizzling flesh to dried bone, dust and ashes, I suddenly found myself facing my own mortality with a profound and total acceptance. The separation which had previously existed between physical life and death was mysteriously cut, and my body was at once filled with an aliveness which seemed to have no beginning, middle or end. A silent aliveness, invisible, inaudible, like a sacred thread of Being uniting this body with all things.

Consequently, I was no longer 'looking at' this death ritual before me. I *was* it. I was *all* of IT, this endless cycle of living and dying. This heaven and hell was of my own creating — the joy, the suffering, the elation, the resignation, and finally, this divine acceptance of ALL THAT IS — ATMAN BRAHMAN.

Some weeks later, back in England, I was sitting in my bedroom, listening to the wind howling outside. I found myself speaking the words, "the body moves, I do *not* move". The more I listened to the wind, the more it entered my body. I *became* the wind. It was as if my body was whispering, "I am wind".

Gradually upsurges of energy began to rise and fall in my body. At first they were like agile undulating waves, then slowly increasing in strength, like the contractions of childbirth, filling and emptying my body from the legs, up through the pelvis, up the spine, and out of my mouth. The sensations experienced in the body were indeed awesome to my ordinary self, but the sacred thread of simplicity remained, and I lay down and allowed Life Itself to live me. Everything and nothing was happening. Any potential attachment to the drama around this situation dissolved, leaving only the awareness of the wind.

Such moments as these have transformed my understanding of my own workshops on the theme of "The Call". What is now clear to me, is that this 'inner call' stems from that place in each of us which is beyond all separation. The instant our sense of separation falls away, we become who we *are*, in truth, the One-in-All-Things. It is the call to this that lies at the heart of my work.

— Chloë Goodchild
Singer and Voice Catalyst

Judith Dawes

Judith Dawes was born, the elder of twins, in 1931 in Sydney, N.S.W. Brought up in the East End of London, she had a career in residential care for children and adults.

In 1954 she became a Christian, first an Anglican, then a Quaker for 20 years, and in 1987 she became a Roman Catholic. She has been active in the peace movement since 1958.

She married Brian in 1962; Joe was born in 1965, Jonathan in 1966, and Ruth in 1968. She divorced Brian in 1986.

She is the author of a book, *Non-Violent God, the Hidden Message.*

Io sono pelegrina a piedi per la pace

(I am a pilgrim walking for peace)

It wasn't the first pilgrimage I'd made. The other was with my husband from whom I'd just been divorced. I was carrying the grief of that, and the freedom. Francis had always been special to us in the same way a couple share a piece of music.

Retracing the steps of an inspired pilgrim fifty years before, I was caught up in our mutual love of this *jongleur de Dieu*. I carried very little — my intention, and the longing that the church would take up its vocation to strive for peace and to cherish the earth.

I had walked out of Assisi through a little-used gate, across an olive grove and along a quiet road to the church of St. Damiano, which Francis had restored, where he had conversed with Christ through the crucifix above the altar, and to which Clare had come to the cloistered life constrained on her by the tradition of that time.

As I continued on my way, it seemed they came together with me. You know when you go to stay with friends, they take you to everything that's important for them, lovely and fun... As I journeyed under the hot sun in that pastel-coloured landscape, I walked into festivals and vibrant celebrations of the mass.

I came to the ancient living springs of Cliturno. They form deep clear pools and a fast flowing river. Francis must have refreshed his body and soul here on his way to war and, soon after, passed them again returning to Assisi and his true mission.

Each approaching nightfall brought the insecurity of a possible night without shelter or food. I was seldom refused. I was given hospitality in the wide vale of Spoleto and in the high places round the small Vale of Rieti, which had been so vital to Francis, and even more sanctified by 800 years of pilgrims' prayers.

In the caves where he had found shelter and solitude, as I meditated on what had happened to him there, and on my own state of being, I experienced tremendous cleansing through tears and radiant joy. So often, familiar words which I couldn't trace came to mind: 'the doves who hide in the clefts of the rock'.

To live so simply, dependent on others' nurturing, drew me very close to the elements and the creatures and people we shared them with, especially the children. I seldom ate a midday meal in a village without the company of such as Simona, and Flavius, and their cat, unabashed by their curiosity and our mutual giggles and limited conversation.

On the steep hillside of Poggio Bustone, I met an old woman in black who, it seemed, wordlessly heard and responded to my mission. In the evening the women knitting together at the top of the village invited me to sit with them before many of us went down to mass. And all the time I was half conscious of a man who had come near us, the stem of a carnation held between his lips — a mixed gesture of clowning and reverence.

One early morning, I wandered almost unwillingly into a large opulent church, drawn by the sunlight streaming through the stained glass windows onto an open bible. I saw the word *roccia*. It was a moment of delight — the most noble trysting.

Alzati, amica mia,
Mia bella, e vieni
O mia colomba, che stai nelle
Fenditure della roccia...

Come then my love,
My lovely one, come.
My dove hiding in the clefts of the rock
In the coverts of the cliff,
Show me your face,
Let me hear your voice, for your voice is sweet
And your face is beautiful.

Song of Songs, Ch. 2, V. 14

With such tenderness Francis had embraced the leper.

— Judith Dawes
Peace Worker and Pilgrim

Kamala Raymakers

My name is Kamala Raymakers, born the 17th of April in 1955.

I live in Bergen, a lovely green village on the coast in the North of Holland. I work mainly at home, exploring the fields of art, music, theatre and healing.

'Breathe...'

After a long period of introspection, inward seeking, journeying, where nothing seemed to come to birth, and a growing financial pressure, I found myself in a crisis again... comparing myself with others, questioning my role in the world, questioning the decisions I had taken for myself, my life... I found no answer and turned to my guide Bertrand: "What do you think of it?" And he answered...

Have the courage
To listen to the silence,
Instead of man-made laws.

Have the courage
To wait,
Instead of hunting.

To receive,
Instead of grasping.

To find,
Instead of searching.

And breathe, breathe, breathe.

and I knew...
things were all right...

— Kamala Raymakers
Singer

Christopher Greatorex

Christopher Greatorex is a psychotherapist living near Stroud, Gloucestershire. He runs workshops on relationships, and is passionate about bringing the human face back into the field of medicine, offering courses for health professionals in Medical Synthesis.

The Labyrinth

A major life experience invites, if not guarantees, a visit to the underworld and an encounter with the gods who live there, whom we put there and whom we would rather stay there. Most of us do not risk a meeting with Dionysus, let alone a confrontation with Ereshkigal, so Life itself will set these matters up for anyone who is actually interested in Living.

It was during 1979, after surgery, radiotherapy and chemotherapy, themselves almost designed to open doors to the nether regions, that I embarked on the first of a series of psychotherapy sessions. This involved my going up to London by train and travelling to Swiss Cottage (one of those quaint London place names that evokes a feeling of cosiness and simplicity, and which has absolutely no connection with reality). As I was fairly disabled, I went from Paddington to my appointment by taxi the first two or three times and then, encouraged, I began to negotiate the Tube, the underworld of London.

Travelling in the underworld of the underground is a curious experience at the best of times. Most of us take it rather for granted when the excitement wears off and learn to switch off to the movement, the noise, the swell, and read the advertisements of other people's papers, anything to avoid making eye contact with a stranger. It must be agony for claustrophobics.

Who would have thought that I would meet my Waterloo on the Bakerloo at Paddington. Not I. It happened thuswise:

I had found my way down to the northbound platform slowly but surely. I always allowed plenty of time because I walked with a stick, the kind that has a big black rubber bit on the end which stops the stick from slipping; the kind that old people have when they get a bit infirm. The platform was crowded, as if there had not been a train for some time. I stood and waited.

You always know when a train is coming long before you hear it. There is a subtle movement of air before the draught, the rush of wind and the roar of this approaching monster of the underworld. I had never felt fear on the Tube before, but this time I was aware of my anxiety. The doors opened, everyone crowded in and took the remaining seats. The rest stood, including myself, for being rather slow, I had climbed on last. I looked around: no seat. This would be a test of my physical stability. I clung onto a metal post and stuck my stick in between the wooden slats. The doors shut and the train moved slowly out of Paddington.

After less than a minute, I noticed someone beginning to stand up, although the next station was a long way off. She was a small white-haired woman all of 70 (I was 40) who caught my eye and pointed out her seat, motioning me towards it. She, amongst all the other passengers, was offering me her seat. I was flabbergasted. More than that, my pride was up against it, and I was very tempted to refuse. How could I take this gesture from this elderly lady, in public, everybody watching, what will they think, how dare she expose me, humiliate me thus? All of this went on in about two seconds. I blurted a quick "thank you very much" and stumbled to the seat.

As I sat down I felt as if my heart had been impaled on a meat hook, like the dead body of Inanna. I blushed, not that anyone would have noticed under my long hair and beard. My breathing was short and shallow, not that anyone would have heard above the noise of the train. Tears welled up in my eyes, not that anyone would have seen from behind their newspapers.

The pain in my heart was not steel, neither hook, nor dagger, though wounded I certainly was. A deep wound, perhaps the deepest of all, the wound of Love. How much I had experienced love before then I do not know. Certainly I had never allowed myself to *receive* such love before. We bandy the phrase 'unconditional love' about as if it were something to acquire or attain, something we should express or have, and as something which is better than personal love. This was something else. This was a gift, both personal and unconditional. A recognition of infirmity and limitation, an acknowledgement of suffering and vulnerability, of human frailty.

Not until that moment, I think, had I really accepted and experienced my own frailty and dependency. Never before had I felt so utterly accepted and bereft, both at the same time.

As I alighted at Swiss Cottage, I looked around for the unlikely bearer of my gift, more precious than anything the Three Kings could have borne, but she was gone, swallowed up by the labyrinthine twists and turns of underground passages and tunnels. Dazed though I was, I made my way to the station entrance and out into the London air. I felt different, I was different. Something new was born in me, and not without pain. Is there any birth without pain? I had descended into the underworld, and I had returned. I had met an old woman. She had me impaled.

— Christoph Greatorex
Transpersonal Therapist and Cook Par Excellence

Diana Lodge

Diana Lodge was born in 1906 of Welsh parents, and spent her childhood there until she went to Bristol University.

After teaching a few years, she went on the stage until she married the poet Oliver Lodge in 1932. She had three children (Belinda, Tom and Colin).

In 1955 Diana's husband died, and ten years later she entered the Roman Catholic Church.

Diana has had painting exhibitions in Washington, Puerto Rico and England. She has been living and painting in the Cotswolds since 1946.

One Foot in Eden

If anyone should ask me what was the happiest time of my life, I would tell them of three weeks I spent on a rock island in the Irish Sea, cut off from the mainland by six miles of a fierce tidal race.

The island had been a shrine of pilgrimage since the 6th Century, when a Celtic monastery was founded there by refugee monks from Brittany. In the 13th Century it was replaced by an Augustinian Abbey, the ruins of the Tower still stand, and nearby is a cross bearing the inscription that twenty thousand saints are buried there, a holy island! There is a Presence on that island.

I had been lent a one-roomed cottage; the only furniture, a table, a chair and a mattress laid across the beams in the rafters, reached by a ladder; no electricity or plumbing.

In front of the cottage, little stone walled fields swept down to the sea, grazed by sheep and geese. Behind, a mountain rose five hundred feet dropping steeply to a rough passage where seals swam in the deep waters. Rough winds and salt spray had swept the island bare of trees.

There were two small farms on the island and a few bird watchers, but I rarely met anyone. I would wander all day, just Being, lying like a seal on a rock, or reading in a field under the lee of a stone wall. I had taken two books, the Bible and the Cloud of Unknowing. I had no clock or radio, no contact with the world.

It was as if one's spirit were a pool, turbulent and muddy with the pace and distractions of the world. In this solitude the mud sank slowly to the bottom and the clear water reflected the sky. When I had to leave I felt I had been turned out of Paradise. Back in the world again I could hardly get up in the morning to realise I had lost Eden. My family said, "You are like a woman who has left her lover."

Last September, I found myself near this coast again. I drove along and saw the Island shining in the distance. I sat on the top of the cliff and felt the old spell drawing me to it.

Why not? I thought, I could take another week off. It was later in the year than my former idyllic experience, and it might turn cold and I had only summer clothes. But I could take a chance for a few days. I enquired at a farm and found there was an empty cottage I could have for a week, it was already closed up for the winter.

I waited for hours in the lonely fisherman's cove, until he arrived and picked me up and dumped me in the little boat; we bounced forward onto the open sea. As we rounded the cliff at the end of the cove,

77

the Island rose up dark in the distance against the western sky, a threat or a promise?

Some have found it a threat. A young Pole lived the hermit life and was eventually carried off screaming in a strait jacket.

Now I was back. I walked to my house by the sea at the far end. Slowly in the remembered peace, I felt the island take possession of me. No sound but the sea and the sheep and the seals singing their eerie, almost human, chants. Autumn came the next day.

As before, I lived with the sun, climbing the mountain at dawn to watch the sun rise over the distant blue ranges of the mainland, and again in the evening to see it sink into the western sea. It wasn't warm enough to lie about as on my first visit, though I found sheltered spots where I could draw. If the wood I brought home was too damp to burn I sat up in bed, hugging the hot water bottle the farmer's wife had thoughtfully offered me, reading or writing, by candlelight. At the end of the week I cleaned up and packed and went down to the beach in the early cold to wait for the boat. I was ready to go, it was late in the year for these camping conditions. The weather had broken.

And then the fisherman arrived to say no boat could cross as the wind had changed to the southeast, the sea was too rough.

I felt wonderfully in God's hands to go or stay, with no option and therefore no will in the matter. So I left my luggage in the fisherman's shed and walked around the shore. I was quite content to stretch my rations for a day or two.

But when the wind stayed in the wrong direction for days, the sun disappeared and my canvas shoes were full of holes and always wet, I wanted to go. I was cold and hungry all the time. I decided to meet this situation by not building hopes on getting away but accepting imprisonment and enjoying it.

The sun came out and the island was beautiful in its wild winter mood. The wind had gone mad and the sea roared like an express train. The furious sea and screaming wind possessed the island, the waves threw themselves to the top of the great jagged black cliffs, and would then boil and foam in the chasms below. The seals watched me with their dark limpid eyes. They weren't singing anymore but diving and swimming in the terrifying water.

I returned to my cottage and my solitude and my meagre rations. I had collected mushrooms and blackberries and the farmer's wife spared me a loaf of her baking.

Life became a physical struggle and my whole body responded to this as if there is a deep need here that never gets satisfied in our comfortable modern age. I was learning 'less is more', and 'I had one foot in Eden'.

I remembered reading Wilfred Thesiger's *Arabian Sands* — how something in him responded to the harsh life of the desert and how he said, when the plane took him away from Arabia, "I knew what it was to go into exile". I felt terribly well and filled with a deep peace. So when after three weeks I was told that the wind had changed, and if I was on the shore the next morning at 7:00 AM, I might get off, I had mixed feelings!

I crossed the Island for the last time in the dark of the dawn. The little boat took us across the smooth sea, now mild as a sheep. As I stepped onto the mainland, I took off the remains of my canvas shoes and threw them out to sea. They sank, and I turned and walked reluctantly up the port through the cove. I was grateful for the glimpse... but back into exile.

— Diana Lodge
Painter

Yvan Rioux

Yvan Rioux was born in Montreal in 1945. He has a degree in Biology from Montreal University, and he practised bio-dynamic farming in Quebec for ten years.

For four years he taught anatomy and occult physiology to adults in alternative medical trainings, such as homoeopathy.

He is currently working with a colleague in The Live Water Trust, creating a lab and an aquatic nursery of plants that can digest toxins in water, as a natural antidote to pollution on a domestic and industrial scale.

He *hasn't* written a book.

This Strange Phenomenon of Jealousy

Several disappointments gave rise to a great sadness in my soul and led me, in my twenties, to close the door on sexual attraction. When I look at this time from the vantage of age, I think that I arranged romantic situations where the response would be 'no'. Then came the great melancholy. This chaos allowed me to explore poetry, to begin to write, to sublimate by studying, to open myself to inner movements and to love nature passionately and be close to it.

At the start of my thirties, having thrown out all rules of conduct, the burning experience of jealousy began. My first experiences with women were actually openings to other realms. We slept with those we were drawn to and talked about it openly. Very soon I was confronted with this strange phenomenon of jealousy — this sudden misery and anger that invaded my life. When there is a great unknown like this, you can feel great anger or abandon your woman with bitterness. When it is a question of your best friend, then it is even thornier. You love a being with all your might, believing that it will go on. You love with the best that is in you (at least that is what you think) and this being, for a time or forever, says 'no' to you.

This feeling of jealousy led to self depreciation. It led to hate/vengeance. What is it that impelled me to live these fraught situations, even to provoke them sometimes? It is hard to say. One thing is sure: once I am in the throes of pain I can not draw back. I must find a new equilibrium. After having gone through a lot of chaos in my twenties for ten years, I suddenly understood that, at bottom, nothing belongs to us. There is in jealousy an old depth of animal instinct probably very healthy for the strengthening of the species. An instinct tied to territory and possessiveness. There is also the fear of being ridiculed (your image takes a tumble), the feeling of being dispossessed of your day. There is a longing for the womb where everything is absorbed, and a tendency to refuse to examine yourself (she is wrong, it is not my fault). It is so hard to change our tracks of feeling and thinking.

I realised, too, that the power I thought I had over others (the power of seduction — I am irreplaceable) enslaves more than it liberates me. Who is more prisoner — the prisoner or the guard?

A lot of things we think we possess do not really belong to us — not even our children, and certainly not the woman who accompanies us. Things are lent to us so that we can help them evolve. It does not matter what can be taken away from us — even our physical body. Jealousy in my life brought me close to the prospect of death.

What peace
What lightness
    when all that mounted in me as great proof.
Jealousy is always there
    it can crush me
    or I can simply tame it
    like some old thing, very old,
    that no longer has any validity.

My life lightened
unglued from things:
I no longer wished to own anything
and especially not to define myself
by what I 'owned'.
From then on my life felt richer
    for this freedom.

        I am born
        of a better day
        when princes
        are no longer prisoners
        of the abuse of power.

— Yvan Rioux
Biologist and Teacher

Carolyn Askar

Born in London, she is a performance poet, actress, drama lecturer, voice teacher and creative therapist. She is joint organiser of the Angels of Fire Poetry Performance Group and also performs her own work solo throughout the U.K. and abroad. She has published three collections of poetry.

The Mountain in Perspective

at the top there
a view of
the world   are

halfway up   no
the view below
gives courage. mountains

at the beginning   only
of the ascent
insurmountable   troughs
but challenging.

         out

at the foot
daunting   of
and overpowering.

         which

closer
awe-inspiring
and imposing.   to

In the distance
majestic.   rise.

— Carolyn Askar

Lizzie Spring

Lizzie Spring is a pianist and performance poet. Her most recent collection of poems, *First Things*, was published by the Diamond Press in 1987.

She continues to balance writing, composing and painting, while embarking upon the practice of holistic massage and aromatherapy.

'In that six months I would ... uncover my life'

The whole day passed clear but at an unfeelable, untouchable distance, as if I had been encased in perspex. I did all that was normally done: feeding the ducks and chickens; hoeing the vegetable patch; walking the dog; answering my husband's questions under the bright sun. All as if the shock had shifted me a millimetre out of earth's space and time. This could be seen by no one and I could not speak of it.

The relief of bedtime, with the chance to drop this ghastly facade of normality, was soon succeeded by the realisation of the impossibility of rest: incapable of lying quietly, shock reverberating in the gut; all electrodes in the head fusing; unable to register anything except the existence of the shock.

I slid out of bed, leaving the man breathing gently. Putting on sensible shoes; gliding downstairs; clipping on the dog's lead: all actions performed with the slow unstoppable deliberation of an automaton.

The dog, although excited to be out at this time of night, was also restrained. In those days I used to be frightened by the dark to the point of terror; yet here I was, walking up the track to the head of the valley in that thick tangible darkness one experiences in the nights before the new moon. We went steadily up to the curve in the track where I stopped and turned.

On this dark night of no stars, the black blue of the sky pressed on my mouth and eyeballs, in my nostrils and ears; it lay over the trees which seemed to hover above the sheer black space that I knew to be water where even the coots were quiet.

Suddenly, although thoroughly aware of where I was standing, I could see a long way off, beyond planets, where it was light. Streaming light and an awe-ful kindness. Bright flowers and fresh grass.

In that instant I understood that the whole of my life as an anxious, earnest, conscientious and hard-working person was as nothing. I had done and tried to do all the things which other people and I thought I ought and could and should do; but I had done nothing towards the purpose for which I was here. (That should have been an alien thought, having thought God to be some kind of patriarchal, autocratic fiction to terrify people into submission.) I now knew myself to be far off centre, the centre of what I existed to become, and that the becoming would be more a matter of exposure than of construction.

Six months to live? I felt that this disease inside was not cancer but whatever it was didn't matter, that was irrelevant. The reality was that, even if I had only six months, in that six months I would throw all caution to the winds and uncover my life, live as fully as I had never dared so far in my thirty three years to date. I knew that (whatever happened, whoever was disappointed in me) the honest purpose — unguessable from the outside maybe — would emerge.

Somewhere a cow coughed, the spring water splashed, the stream ran on and the dog lay patiently beside me in the dark.

Curiously, I have no memory at all of the immediate succeeding events. Did my husband wake up? Did we talk of this? I simply do not remember. Seven years later my life is radically different, although I am still in the dark as to my purpose. However, that moment on the hillside is a touchstone for me. I know I am on my journey and whenever I feel I am in the 'wrong' place or doing the 'wrong' thing, I feel back to the immediacy of that night, testing my distance from the centre. If there is a sense of wasted life and immediacy of death with life unfulfilled, then I know I am going cold and need to change direction.

— Lizzie Spring
Musician

Ronald Higgins

Ronald Higgins is a former sociologist, former diplomat, former journalist and present Director of the Dunamis Open Forum at St. James's Church, Piccadilly, W.1.

He wrote *The Seventh Enemy* (1982) and *Plotting Peace* (1990), amongst other things. He is Chairman of the Champernowne Trust, and vice-chairman of the Herefordshire Community Health Trust.

But mainly he cultivates his garden and breeds ducks.

Break-through

If there was a single crucial moment in my own break-through — or break-out! — it happened at, of all occasions, a fat lunch party at a West End advertising agency.

So crucial did it prove for my pattern of life that I seem hardly to have had so good a lunch again. Good winds sometimes blow ill?

At the time I was working in a senior position at *The Observer*. Among other things I had charge of the newspaper's promotion. The lunch was to celebrate our staying ten years with the same agency — an unusually long haul in the rough waters of Fleet Street.

I was the third member of a discussion between David Astor, the then editor, and the smooth, bright, sharp managing director of the agency. The latter was asked by Astor whether he saw an early resumption of the economic boom after the current (and first) oil price crisis was sorted out. It must have been 1974 — OPEC had just administered a seismic shock to old expectations.

Or so I had thought. The managing director, however, blandly answered Astor that all would be well. Growth would be resumed; affluence, consumption, profitability would soon again soar. There would be an ever-better tomorrow.

I heard myself explode with anger and amazement. Did he not realize the sheer pace of the population explosion, the gathering food crisis, the degradation of the environment, the spread of nuclear danger? Did he not see how Rich North and Poor South were being ever more bitterly divided by a *growing* poverty gap? And how catastrophically inadequate was the human response to this convergent set of challenges? Look at the pathetic performance of the U.N., at the parochiality and nationalism of most governments — leave aside the potentially fatal East-West conflict? Surely we had to recognize that the oil price crisis and the rest were but early symptoms of what could prove to be an enduring crisis, a climacteric, for all humanity? (I'd never spoken like this before: I was as surprised as he.)

I can't remember what he replied. Perhaps another course was served, or the talk turned to our next television commercial. In the taxi back to the office, however, David Astor asked me to write a long piece in *The Observer Colour Magazine*. Soon afterwards I took boxes of books and journals down to a friend's cottage in the Alpes Maritimes and gradually hacked out a rather doom-laden article called "The Seventh Enemy" and sub-titled "Is the world committing suicide?"

When it came out in February 1975, we got 7000 letters mostly saying something like 'thank God someone is spelling it out.' The book then followed (Hodder and Stoughton published the latest edition in January 1982) and then BBC *Everyman* made a film about its writing — in my own cottage in Herefordshire's Golden Valley. In 1980 I went entirely free-lance — writing and lecturing about the urgent need for more generous, or at least more intelligent, international relationships. Within five years my life had turned upside down (and was now perhaps the right way up!).

Yet the original moment was, I think, in retrospect, only the sudden birth of a child within; a child that had been gestating for many years. Twelve years of service as a British diplomat had clearly had much to do with it. Over those years I had gradually come to realise how horrifically intractable international relations are. It is like trying to stir semolina with a feather. Then followed eight years in Fleet Street during which I realised how public opinion is often almost as intractable. Yes, you can give currency to a new idea, a new movement: to a new personality certainly! If a journalist wants to tackle root issues of international life or values or the likely global outcomes of short term thinking, he is very likely to lose the public's attention — and perhaps his job! Fundamentals are not news. Nor are they especially entertaining. Nor, of course, is the preacher.

It was, however, those two long experiences of how things are done (or not done) by governments, and of how the public generally prefers it that way, that led to my outburst. The sceptical view of human responses to what should be obvious challenges must have been intensified by the contrast between the naive optimism with which I had entered the Foreign Office in 1954, and the gradual discovery of feet of clay, not only of the headline names I was working amongst, but attached to my then pin-striped and rather portly body.

For me, at least, a troubled marriage followed and a posting to Indonesia with which Britain was then at war over in Borneo, and which itself had recently barely survived a vicious and murderous civil war. It should be sufficient to say that the conjunction of these harrowing events drove home on me the acute vulnerability of all relationships and of all patterns of order. They instructed my heart with harrowing effect.

I became much more live to the power of unconscious elements in life, including, of course, those in my own behaviour. Indeed there was more suffering, and more learning, to come, especially in the three gruelling years it took me to write *The Seventh Enemy*. Some of this was no doubt the result of the long periods of solitude. Not only ideas but emotions started whirling in a kind of vortex. Perspective is lost and the lack of contact with the trials — and the humour — of others tended in me at least to generate an alternation of emotional depression and intellectual over-ambition. Was I a failure or a saviour? The truth, of course, was neither.

Yet whatever various processes of heart or head were operating during these years I have little doubt about the power of one particular moment — for both heart and head. You will recall that I had long since concluded that the human outlook was abysmal unless there was swift, self-sacrificial and radical change in the behaviour of governments. But that change could only happen if there was also a startling change in the perceptions and priorities of public opinion at large.

This would be possible only if numerous individuals made it their business to bring it about. How? By appealing to more generous values, and common interest in global stability, but also perhaps to a larger sense of human providence.

Fate seemed to have cast me into this uncomfortable tribe, in however small a role. In comparison with the immensity of the task, my own impact was bound to be puny. Did the abandonment of orthodox life, secure salary, predictable outcomes of any sort, really make sense? Was it something rooted not in my realities but in a crazy mini-Messiah fantasy? Could I ever justify the break-out in instrumental terms of people persuaded, results achieved? What really was the point of even trying?

At this bad stage I wandered up the lane one morning to collect my newspaper and found my neighbour Bill Taylor, a retired forestry worker, sadly surveying the ruins of his stone and timber woodshed which had collapsed in a storm overnight. He looked up as I arrived and grinned rather shyly. There was a silence. Then he said: "Oh well, Ron, you'll be knowing all about this I reckon. These things be sent to try us."

Even a cliché can sometimes create a moment of astonishment and magic. What struck home was Bill's obvious awareness that I'd been going through a hard time and his shy (and correct) recognition that he wouldn't understand the arguments that had been swirling in my over-educated head. But nevertheless he had by instinct reminded me of a staggeringly simple set of truths — that we understand little of what happens; that we do not and cannot control much of what happens in life; that we cannot ourselves judge the significance of our actions; that in large part it is almost impious and hubristic to attempt it.

Bill's familiar phrase was lifted from the level of casual chat on a windy hill to that of a delicately stated understanding of a profound truth. The moment has stayed in my memory because it brought me down from lonely and rather pretentious philosophising into the humbler, perhaps holier, place where we both recognise and celebrate our ordinariness.

For some time after I'd finished the book, I immersed myself in working in the field of emotional and personality disorders by running the network of therapeutic communities established by the excellent Richmond Fellowship founded by Elly Jansen.

We can come to grips with the large events only by grappling with the individual human soul and not least perhaps by working out from its 'ordinariness'. Much of the social therapy at the Fellowship happens over, say, the sink. It is about self discipline, self respect, eye-to-eye contact, what is happening now between you and me.

As I write this, years later, in mid-January, the orchard is thigh deep in snow and only an hour ago I was hacking out a narrow path up our ancient lane with the help of our neighbour Bill Taylor. He didn't mention that these things are sent to try us. He knows I know, now.

— Ronald Higgins
Catalyst for change on the economic
and nuclear fronts,
Founder of Dunamis, St. James's Piccadilly
and author of *The Seventh Enemy: The Human
Factor in the Global Crisis, Plotting Peace:
The Owl's Reply to the Hawks and Doves*, and
Infertility: New Options, New Dilemmas (with
his second wife, Dr. Elizabeth Bryan)

Rhoda Cowen

Rhoda Cowen was born in 1909. She is a wife, mother and grand-mother.

On A Northumberland Moor

We were married in the height of the blitz in London. John was terrified of the bombs after his campaign in the North African desert (where he never slept under a roof for four years). He was brought back to train for the European invasion; we had a weekend honeymoon and only met in snatches before D-day and then he was abroad for three years. At last he came home and we moved to Northumberland, his home, to start our married life.

We were both physically, mentally, and spiritually exhausted and greatly disturbed, and it was hard and perplexing. The months passed. Northumberland is grand and grey — magnificent sweeping panoramas — but for me from the south, there was no springtime or delicate primrose. Winter slid imperceptibly into summer and golden autumn. There was little intimacy or magic. I had very few friends, fewer kindred spirits. The neighbours' lives had been relatively undisturbed by the war. They still had servants, cream and sugar in their after-dinner coffee, and eight hours undisturbed sleep in their own beds — all inconceivable and unfamiliar to me.

The first years of our marriage were not easy. One afternoon I walked up on the moors. Curlews calling, grouse scurrying. Truly a Gethsemane, a deliberate confrontation. I said over and over again the marriage vows I had made before God.

I take thee John ... for better, for worse ... till death do us part.

And Shakespeare's Sonnet No. CXVI:

Let me not to the marriage of true minds
Admit impediments. Love is not love
which alters when it alteration finds,
Or bends with the remover to remove:
O no! It is an ever-fixed mark
That looks on tempests and is never shaken;
...
Love alters not with his brief hours and weeks,
But bears it out even to the edge of doom.

How to come to terms with living in the north? Its loneliness and frustrations? And I repeated:

Not my will, but Thy will be done.

And here I offer to Thee myself, my soul, and my body... to be a living sacrifice.

Some time later I went back to feed the baby, deeply at peace. During the feed John arrived back from a day in London. His chairman had offered him a huge promotion in Head Office. The question was now: shall we go back to London and start a new life together?

Postface

I suppose I have always known God, and that God is Love, and perhaps that is the greatest blessing a soul can be granted for its earthly incarnation. I have doubts about who and what God is, and how to worship Him and what to do about it all, but a basic certainty has always been there.

I have also known that any deviation from Love is man's work, not God's, and that it is in the divine plan for man to be given free will. How he handles any given situation is his own choice, whether from the highest motive or not, and that this earthly life is a training ground for each soul and for humanity. Any straying from the divine plan is man's choice, not God's. The vital link between God and man is the Christ, of whom Jesus of Nazareth was one of the supreme manifestations. So-called misfortune comes to us, often through our own actions or as part of the pattern of our lives, or karmic consequences, but never at random.

Looking back on my life span I perceive a golden thread running right through, woven into the extraordinary tapestry of its events and experiences. A golden thread, which I call the Love of God, a guiding hand, often invisible at the moment, but in hindsight, unmistakable.

— Rhoda Cowen
Teacher in Africa and China

'The Light, the Light! The Heart-Delighting Light!'

– Lord Byron

Sir George Trevelyan

Sir George Trevelyan was born in 1906. After Cambridge, he was an apprentice furniture maker for two years in Chalford, Glos. He still sleeps in the walnut bed he made 65 years ago.

Honoured for services in the Home Guard, he was later Founder and Warden of the first adult education centre at Attingham Park, Shropshire. Courses were offered here on every conceivable subject – birdsong, heraldry – and then on a new spirituality, centred on the teaching of Rudolf Steiner.

In 1971 he founded the Wrekin Trust, mounting courses for spiritual education all over England. Ten years later he began to lecture abroad – on the continent, in the U.S. and in South America.

Sir George is a thinker, educator, mountaineer and craftsman, and a courageous spokesman for evolutionary education, abroad and at home.

Here Now

It came to me on February 5, 1990 at 2 AM. In the days before, I had been finding that, at the moment of waking in the wee hours, my mind held light in it, and a phrase or affirmation, a statement of great clarity. It was no use trying to remember, since the precious thing faded like a dream unless caught immediately. So I kept pencil and paper beside me.

When I went to bed on the 4th, I asked my Higher Self and Angelic Guide to allow me to go through into ethereal space consciously, as in the near-death experience. That proved to be asking too much; but, instead, they gave me an experience that was truly an *epiphany* event.

I know with deep and direct certainty that God is Life, wherever it manifests. He is Spirit in action. He IS, as I AM. He IS in me and you. That means we are each a divine droplet of the same vast Being which is Humanity. Christ is the Love aspect of God. The rising tide of Love which we recognise and accept now IS Christ in manifestation. Thus God can blend with us and speak to us *in our own thinking*, and the Christ-Love can flood our hearts if we will but open to it. My Higher Self and Angelic Guide would not allow me the continuity of consciousness in sleep, but veritably I believe they gave me this experience for my encouragement...

I woke and was all joy. I felt — 'This is IT." Without qualification, this is the JOY. I live in it this instant with heart aglow. This is the timeless moment, this moment in God — as God. He has put us through all the trouble to get HERE NOW. Rest in this moment in total acceptance — me in Him, He in me. I am home — at last. All is One. We are each conscious droplets of Divinity. You and I are the same God Being. We are One, One vast Being of God. I AM HOME. This is IT. A total stillness and total Joy in Love. I can criticize nobody. I can love everybody, however improbable. Total forgiveness, total acceptance. Since we are all droplets of the One, our aberrations should be lovable. There is no need for criticism or fault-finding.

There is nothing but the NOW moment, and in it I am in direct touch with the Christ-Love which, like a rising tide, is seeping and flooding everywhere. This Christed state, this God power in me, is the Goal reached, the Presence. I may lose it again in the tangles of the coming day, but now I AM there. I have arrived. All that I have been through leads to NOW, this Present Moment. The Presence.

It was as if I'd left my body and was melted into Him, the

Christ-Heart, the Light. Complete protection. I am still involved with earth body, and I know that at dawn I shall rise to the affairs of a new day and its concerns. But NOW — I AM — HE IS. This room is full of Him. His Light floods through everything and through me. This is sheer joy. Everything is lovable and right.

I know heart-sympathy for each being in its endearing ways or limitations, in its irritation or anger, its hate, fear, criticism. Nothing touches or disturbs the peace, serenity, loving joy, sympathy, forgiveness, fun, that fills each moment and contact. There is no haste or hurry. You, Lord Christ, Lover, Lord, Friend — I have reached You after so long through the valleys of separation. This is the Goal now reached.

My task is to make this continuous until the wonderful day when I shall be released into the Light. This experience is indeed:

A condition of complete simplicity
(Costing not less than everything)
And all shall be well
And all manner of thing shall be well
When the tongues of flame are infolded
Into the crowned knot of fire
And the fire and the rose are One

—   T.S. Eliot
'Little Gidding', *Four Quartets*

— George Trevelyan

Stephanie Melliar-Smith

Stephanie Melliar-Smith was born in England on September 21st 1948. She went to Edinburgh University, and then went to live in Spain (Seville) in 1971.

For twenty years she has lived in Andalucia and Madrid, earning a living from teaching and translating. She has always painted.

She has one son, Miguel.

'Who knows what
may arise?'

When I was thirteen, I had a dream of Christ on a mountain. I went up close and he gave me his hand and filled me with great electricity, an energy of promise and white light. It was strange because then I had never read any religious books, or taken any interest in the subject. But I did not forget that transmission.

Only too often I am faint-hearted and bound up in little things, in plans and ego-weaving games. Matter weighs me down, and I wonder how I could let so much gloom into my life after the great help I've been given.

But meditation is wonderful here. It stops me falling into that death forever. I began meditating at university because of a love that wasn't returned. So mad was I for this friend that I'd go to any lengths to share his world; at that time he was a philosopher, and I expect he still is. He mentioned Buddhism. I found a group in Edinburgh that really fired me — so much happened in ten days with the Thai monks. First, for three days there was a terrible stench. How could everything smell like that? and seem to emit a kind of viscosity? The monk said it was 'the disgusting phase'. Then I felt terrible fear, never before or since like this. And, in the end, the greatest peace imaginable, with no counterpart.

I left in a hurry, though, as I had made up my mind to kill myself. The monk asked me to stay, but I couldn't: I felt I should kill myself, as I had seen the soldiers die in the jungle in Vietnam. I felt I'd finished my life. In fact, I'd gone through pregnancy and old age in the meditation.

But offering up this gloom or fury is all. When I'm in the middle of it, it seems impossible to lay aside, but Chogyam Trungpa teaches gentleness, and when I can see the fear and recoil, it makes new worlds sounding of far-off times and places slip in instead.

And now, though really I have nothing special to say, I know there are so many great ones who speak to the heart. They come during the day (or night) through friends, and the unveiling of the Shambala kingdom comes from ordinary daily contact with people. And this can flood the world with fresh air and laughter — who knows what may arise?

— Stephanie Melliar-Smith
Computer Operator and Translator

Mary Wykeham

Mary Wykeham was born in 1909; she is a painter, engraver, nun and hermit. Distanced by politics from her family, she studied art in London, Berlin and Paris, and learned engraving at Hayter's Atelier. Periods of blindness interrupted her work. She produced portfolios – 'Salvo for Russia' and illustrated *The Secret of the Golden Flower*. She exhibited in Paris and London.

In 1952 she entered a religious order in Aix-en-Provence and discarded the art world. Since 1970 she has lived a solitary life in close touch with the order, and has resumed print-making and painting.

An event that changed
a life...

*By collecting the thoughts, one can fly,
and will be born in heaven.*

*That which exists through itself
is called the Way.*

— Tao

In 1948, I made engravings for the eight chapters of *The Secret of the
Golden Flower; a Chinese Book of Life*.

It is a Taoist way of meditating, to arrive at the void, emptiness.

While working on the plates, a desire grew to learn what is meant
by 'heaven', 'the secret within the secret', 'action through non-action'.

Needing to distance myself from my usual surroundings in order to
reflect, when the edition was finished and delivered, I let the studio and
left for Italy with a haversack and no plans, except to look at pictures.

All through Italy one comes face to face with pictures of the
Christian story, which I had known well as a child but stopped believing it was real and gradually came to think God didn't exist.

What follows happened after a long track of reading. I still meditated on the Tao in Sicily in 1949... and painted... and thought of
going to the East to live in an ashram...

Every day as the sun got up, and grey forms became colours, the
spirit rose like mercury, and the body had to get up as well.

Going up the mountain before breakfast seemed like going down
too, into the world's twilight; and every step up over the asphodel-
covered rocks was akin to a descent into the depths of Being. I went
through a hole in a wall, and out onto the bare rocks overlooking the
wide coast-line and snow-capped Etna.

One day in Spring, meditating on the rocks at dawn, using a text of
Eastern wisdom, and enchanted by its poetic beauty, I became aware
that the shapes and colours around me were no longer there, only a dif-
fusion of light that contained them all. The distant sounds of the world
were no longer heard, only complete silence. Names and thoughts disappeared, absorbed in the heart. The stars and the expanse and balance
of the universe were all within, not thought of, but known.

My being was alert, taut like a violin string tuned to the right pitch, ready for the day to play on.

Suddenly, I was filled with joy, aware of an inner certainty of endless being — eternity, rather than immortality. And when the sun rose, like a holy thought, I knew for the first time in thirty years, and without doubt, that God is: and that the face of God is no face, but utter holiness. And that I was nothing.

Then saints and angels seemed to be sailing around, singing among the towering almond trees. My own non-being fell away like a discarded husk, and I was alone yet not alone, but with someone who absorbed me, close yet far away, known yet unknown.

I was convinced that the meaning of life is Being and not nothingness, néant, void or emptiness. All questions seemed to be answered, and the whole to be apparent in each part.

It was a moment of awareness of what is, of reality, a moment of grace, no more than a flash. But I went peacefully back down, certain of God's existence. Although for a time longer reason refused it, the basic certitude remained. And challenged... and life's direction was "changed, changed utterly" (Yeats, 'Easter 1916').

In the autumn of that year I joined the Catholic church, and two years later became a Little Sister of Jesus.

He with whom God is
is never less alone
than when he is alone

— William of St-Thierry

— Mary Wykeham
Nun

Jay Ramsay

Jay Ramsay, born 1958, co-founded the Angels of Fire collective in 1982, and is the project director of Chrysalis – The Poet In You, running courses and workshops here and abroad as well as one-to-one sessions. His main work, *The Great Return*, is a long poem in a series of connected books: others include *The White Poem* – with photographs by Carole Bruce (Five Seasons Press, 1988), *Transformation – the poetry of spiritual consciousness* (Rivelin Grapheme Press, 1988), *Strange Days* (Taxus, 1990), *For Now* – with Geoffrey Godbert (The Diamond Press, 1991), and *Improvisations* (Stride, 1993). He is also the co-translator of the new *Tao Te Ching*, with Martin Palmer and Kwok Man Ho (HarperCollins, 1993).

The Rain, The Rain

When I was a child
My vision was refined in certain skies;
My face is the product of every nuance.

— Rimbaud

I was seven. The room was dark. The room — with its blue walls and blue drawn curtains the summer light would brighten behind... waking to the sound of the mower and the smell of mown grass, waking to light, waking clear and at ease, waking alone, waking happy. At night, the door at the end of the room always stood ajar, and the bed I lay in faced down towards it, and the soft dim glow of the night light that lit the frame of the doorway where the shadow would come — the shadow of a highwayman, black-cloaked, standing there, looking towards me as I struggled against my fear to sleep.

That night I slept easily, without curling up to one side, and with my face uncovered. I lay there on my back and the dark was calm. I hadn't slept long when suddenly I found myself back in my body with a strange surge of energy; and though my eyes were still closed, I was awake, I was more than awake, and I knew that all I had to do was to open my eyes, as I found myself telling myself to — and there it was: filling the whole room, pouring through the ceiling, iridescent through the darkness.

It was rain, and it was light — it was rain, and it was multi-coloured — radiant, glowing, the colours in each droplet interfused across the whole spectrum — falling, dry — pouring, electric — streaming sound- lessly, down to the floor, down over the bed, down over my body; as I closed my eyes and opened them, closed and opened them again, and still it was there. And I let my eyes go into it, and I let myself merge with it — my eyes, the rain, my heart, the rain, and my body — its joy- ous, amazed exultation as I reached up the open palms of my hands.

And at the same time I was calm, I was still: I *knew* it, and I could feel myself watching it — witnessing it without questioning — though how, I couldn't say. Gradually, it receded, after what must have been minutes — and as it did so, and the spaces between its falling dimmed back to darkness, I was drawn back to sleep, sealed in its miraculous certainty, its mystery. Later, when I thought of it, a high sound would enter my inner ear; then it was there, if only for a second, as if it was still raining and always raining.

I told no one, for years. It was my secret joy. As soon as I thought to speak of it, a silence would come over me that was also its own. It was a well to draw on, and I would walk in the feeling of it. I didn't know the name for it, and I didn't need to — I knew it was forever, in itself, unfading. And I knew the difference between it and the cold wet rain of the world, the grey world I was entering: the mechanical world of harshness and fear, exile and loneliness: the alien world, not rain-made, but man-made. And I knew the rain was real as the garden I was leaving with all its sunlight and flowering colours — all its intricate, living detail I had spent hours seeing and being with: the grass, the breeze through the trees, the dappled, green tree — light, the hum of bees and the spread wings of a butterfly poised among vivid petals. I knew the earth was light — the real earth, and I knew that when I saw it was so, I was real as well. I was dreaming awake, and this was what being awake meant — this was what it was and is. It was where I had come from, and it was what I had come to be.

It was my first real life memory. And now? I think back along the tenuous thread of all those I've experienced since, and all that I've written and spoken and shared from them — and this, I see now, is the root of all of them: this rain I've rarely spoken of, and have never written, never named, never explained. I can put a name to it — I can say it was 'rain from heaven', it was 'rainbow rain'; and, gift as it was — coming as it did — it isn't mine to say or mine to claim. It has cloaked me, clothed and fed me where there was no food and my eyes could see nothing. I have left it — but in reality it has never left me. I have betrayed it: but it has never betrayed me. I have been asleep: and always it has woken me, and brought me back to wonder. What do I know? All I know is what I have seen, and been given to see — all I know is gift, is ageless, is given to be given. The rest is history, is process, is ephemeral — shed skins of growth at each turn of the spiral-marker posts along the road of incarnation: this thing we call 'this life', lived by this name, this person.

Are we coming to the end of ourselves now? Beyond all these seas of myth and self we come through — and beyond even the realization that as beings we are multidimensional — there is a new dimension now, both further and far closer, that we are coming to realize we are the direct expression of, that is the colour behind all colours, unknown, all-pervading, all-embracing; that is a mind we can only live by, a heart behind our eyes that seeingly feels through them, and a being, a body that is its bridge and birth. What is closest, deepest, and most unique in us is this — this presence, this present, this 'now' that all time becomes, all the years become, and all our names become. Call it 'rainbow mind', Holy Spirit, Sun — it is, as it will be, all one.

In a flash you see it, it hovers, it holds — you hear words you move to write down, you find a gesture you are making; and beyond emotion it is feeling, fluid, rightness. And it is fire and it is blood. It is air and it is flesh. And isn't that what epiphany means? *The small self eclipsed towards what it truly is?* And isn't it prophecy, too, seeing what is future, and already is, beyond time, coming into time? And isn't that the essence of our lives?

And I hear a voice inside saying 'stay with the rain', and I am there now, letting go there now, and it is the same letting go — and the same downpouring. It is all I wanted to say, and all I wanted to share — beyond all this, its inexhaustible mystery. Beyond these words. The thing itself. So let it rain. The rain from the source. So may it rain on you. The rain, the rain.

And I knew what I still find hard to know — I knew beyond all doubt that I was loved.

— Jay Ramsay
Poet

Gabriel Bradford Millar

I was born in New York in 1944. After Columbia University I wrote a thesis in Edinburgh, where I married an Englishman, published poetry and read on the BBC.

We raised two daughters and some chickens in England, where I wrote three books and gave over 30 readings and workshops ('Down from the Ivory Tower').

For twelve years I have been doing Rhythmical Massage. I live now with my second husband and help him in The Live Water Trust.

Lit and sustained by a few pivotal inner events, I am learning to recognise the Presence, whose spokesmen, impelled by love, abound in the least looked-for places.

I was home after a long time away

It was June 12, 1976. My husband and children and I were at Sherborne House, where a friend was completing her year at the Gurdjieff School; we were with the other guests watching their final performance. Graham was standing at the back, holding our one year-old daughter; our four year-old daughter and I were near the front. The sun streamed down from an unbroken blue sky through the half-timbered building. The movements were meticulously executed to piano music; the students, in white tunics with coloured sashes, moved with savage clarity.

As they chanted *Kyrie eleison*, I felt that we were all outwardly in the passionate grasp of the sun, but that inwardly I was being washed by the warmth and dazzle of something no less urgent, but less physical, beyond and through the sun.

Suddenly, everything around me lit up — everything, everyone was mobile, shifted into levity. There was only this great light holding everyone in it, playing around us. And we were playing in it — it was our home, our element.

I began to cry, and then sob — I felt I was home after a long time away. I sobbed because of the blazing benign power in this light — I had never known this in my life. It was suddenly clear: this was what it was all about — our mottled sojourn here! It was about this love we are so blind to! This divine tenderness that has no measure or end.

The beauty of it... and, *at the same time*, I felt a kind of bitter grief at the fact that we don't see this love and live in it — grief at our blindness and denial. These two things revealed themselves at the same beautiful and terrible moment. My heart cracked open like a nut, and I sobbed as though I would never stop.

It was too much for my body: I fainted and keeled over on the floor. It was probably only a few seconds before I came to and realized what had happened. I got up disoriented, and ran out onto the grass, straight to a big beech tree and lay down. The ground felt cool and unsentimental. It was a comfort, but, it also seemed to deny what had just happened. I felt foolish. I cried different tears now. I put my face in the grass — I felt bereft. I thought, 'I must go back to my girl'.

After what may have been only a few minutes, there seemed to be a hand on my left shoulder. My husband... how good of him, I thought. I looked up — there was no one there.

Then I saw people streaming out onto the lawn, and my family walking towards me. They were all luminous.

Since that morning I have tried to remember the gift of this inconceivable love and to *be* it, to manifest it as mystical fact. I usually fail to do either, but I have met it and I will not forget.

— Gabriel Bradford Millar
Poet and Remedial Therapist

A Lecturer

March Afternoon

I 'knew' this presence would not go away.

The sunshine and pale warmth of a March afternoon filled the room. I looked up from lunch, realising that this was the first light and warmth encountered for a long time. It welled up within the room like a health-giving fountain, until I felt so present to the world that the silence went deep into my heart. It was like a wellspring of health, of life, of strength, which slowly filled my hollowness.

At first I had ignored the atmosphere of silent blessing, preferring my book and meal. But then these fell away like leaves, as if nothing except the light was at all important. As the light gathered, I could see every branch on the trees, the pale blue of the sky, the shadows on the wall in an eternal moment. The images are still with me.

What struck me was the objective quality of the presence — just 'there', in the air, the room, the stirring branches, but also 'here', within me. How long this lasted I cannot say. I remember thinking that if I went outside the experience would go. However, when I did go out, the feelings only deepened into quiet joy, vivid awareness and a growing sense of renewal.

All the while I walked, the hills, streams, rocks, trees, dead bracken and sheep reflected the peace I experienced. The feeling grew stronger, and though I 'knew' this presence would not go away, still I wandered over hills that resonated with peace. I felt a new wild energy and the fatigue of my old self shifting.

I reflected on the years of questioning and searching. The hollow books, the old ways, the waves of demonstrations in the youthful exuberance of 1968, the strange worlds of drugs that had followed for many friends searching for meaning — and my own path, at some sort of end. And then this — a new beginning?

In the months that followed I would occasionally re-enter the still world that had so unexpectedly welled up. Sometimes I would savour a moment as if it were forever. The new beginnings came, haltingly. The wellspring was there — and new courage, life and awareness. And even today, when I feel too 'outward', it's possible to plumb the depths of that presence.

— A College Lecturer

Gudrun Pelham

I love people. I have indeed met all races in the world, having been privileged to live in India, and have sons living in Hong Kong and Africa.

I have seen death in both the very young and the very old. My own husband died, and I died myself, but came back. Death is rather wonderful, but can also be gruesome as I have seen in hospitals. Death is a release. We die many times over, and every time we release something deep, a substantial part of us. There need be no fear, but that is easier said than done for most of us.

May the Light surround us and be in us.

– Gudrun.

Death and Resurrection

My Own Experience

I am Gudrun and I came into this existence 75 years ago. Six months before my birth, my parents lost two small daughters, so my first job was to comfort my father and mother. 'Oh, tidings of comfort and joy.'

I went to school, trained as a nurse and eventually went to India to nurse, paid by a mission society. Once there, I married, gave birth to seven children, all of whom I nursed, plus innumerable other people of different races and ages. I am now settled in England.

At the age of 55, in 1975, at the Royal Berks Hospital in Reading, I 'died' after my third heart attack. The doctor's verdict was simply overwork. I am, however, more alive now in 1989 than ever before. I lead a normal life. What was the real reason for my 'death'? How did 'death' come? And the resurrection!?

Five years before my cardiac arrest ('death'), I consciously started on a path that leads to a complete transformation into Light. Being impatient, impulsive and careless, I finished the prescribed course too quickly. The course is called The Armour of Light and was revealed to and channelled through Olive Pixley, a cousin of my husband. My hunger for Light drove me on.

The summer of '75 was a lovely one, but I did not notice it, consumed as I was with anxiety about my girl who, at seventeen, was involved with relationships and dope. I also looked after a five year-old Nigerian boy who was motherless.

The 9th of July I had my first heart attack and was told to rest, which was impossible, since I had taken on so many tasks. Early morning at 3:00 A.M. on July 16th, I woke with a heart pain which was so severe that I reluctantly had to wake my husband. I needed help to go the toilet. He took me there, but on the way I perceived an immense ball of light that came out of my chest, grew bigger and bigger until I lost consciousness. My poor husband got very frightened, but managed to drag me onto the toilet. He wanted to phone the doctor, but I asked him to wait. The pain might leave. It didn't. So he phoned and I was in hospital before 8:00 A.M.

The ambulance men were lovely, they handled me as if I was made of fine glass. Not so the young doctor in hospital; he made me sit up and palpated my back. I started to glide out through a dark tunnel. The feeling of gliding away was so utterly overwhelming, that there are no words to describe it. I was just about to leave the tunnel, when I was hauled up by my arms and legs in the air. The doctors were taking an X-ray of my heart. I found myself in bed wired up with electric nodes, three of them, and saw my heartbeat on a screen on the wall behind.

The days immediately after I 'died' and was brought back, I don't remember, except that I was in pain. They told me later that I had been given three electric shocks minutes after I passed out. I was beautifully looked after by the hospital staff, but also by angels. I lived naturally on different levels, neither in the past nor the future, but in the present. The pain was a help not a hindrance. As I got clearer into myself I became distinctly aware of my resurrection. That was sealed for me then one morning a week later by the hospital chaplain, who gave me Holy Communion. Everything in the whole experience was very beautiful.

When I was allowed to get up at last and I saw myself in a mirror, I did not recognize myself. It was a young face that looked at me without wrinkles. How strange to be so different! Alas, I did not stay young for long!

I came home and the rehabilitation work began. It was hair-raising. I panicked every time I wanted to move and was unable. It was here that the Armour of Light exercises came into their own. Without them I'm sure I could not have managed. The death experience still clung to me, but now death was not beautiful. I wanted to live. So I did the exercises, visualizing Light coming in like coloured rays into my body in very precise ways. It worked every time. The cramp in my chest dissolved and I could move.

Six months after my death experience I saw the immense Light again. This time it shot through me from head to foot, and I swooned. But instead of a severe heart attack it gave me such energy that I was up and about immediately, elated and happy.

So I learned clearly what Light is and meant to me, and how my heart works. However, I am still learning.

I've been told that my death experience is an initiation, a deep one, and brings with it a great responsibility. I have backslided on my task many times, but basically the Christ Love is in my heart, I know.

— Gudrun Pelham
Mother and Nurse

Valerie Gillies

Valerie Gillies is a poet, freelance writer and tutor. She has taught in schools and a college of art. She writes for BBC radio and television, and for literary and arts reviews. Currently Writer-in-Residence to East Lothian and Midlothian District Libraries, her most recent books of poetry are *Tweed Journey* (1989) and *The Chanter's Tune* (1990), both published by Canongate, Edinburgh. *A Sweet Place* will be published in 1995.

The Moor

Make your way to the moor. You can know more today than its vanished peoples. Here, of all the great hunting-forest, remain a few Scots pines and one slope dusky with oak trees. 3000 years ago those grassy mounds were ancient earthworks; 1000 years ago, this ruin razed to the ground was a fortified tower. In the undrained marshland mosstroopers rode, over warlike centuries. Water was their wine, dried pemmican their food. Farmsteads lie drowned under the vast new reservoirs which supply the cities, and shepherds' cottages up the side glens are a tumble of stones. Every Monday night, shouting is heard, though it is not known who makes the noise. These people left long ago, crossing the surface of an earth that is like a hide scoured clean by flint scrapers.

After winter, the snow-bleached grasses, the wind-flattened reeds stand up again. The heather thickens to the frost nip. The braid of green shoots shows its young beard on the hill. The sound of the icy wind is silenced in the lee of a drystane dyke. The moor has gathered all the past to itself, and renews its youth with rising skylark-song and long bubbling whaup-cry.

Now a child in a tattered leather jacket comes down quickly over the horizon and walks along a known path, running-dog at her heel, mountain-hare in her hand. The lore and the love of the wild hare, the knowledge of its ways and of the secret places where it is always to be found, the risk to life and limb in the solitary following of it, all make the child one with the hunters of the past. And that is what she feels: where she goes, others go with her. Their hunting-calls reply to her in the early morning mists: and at night, if she sleeps out in the open, she hears the stars give their cries.

A quarter of a century passes: a woman brings her youngest child to the moor-crest. The summer bracken is taller than the child, who pushes a way through it. The child calls out, finding a flat boulder with cup-and-ring markings incised on it. The woman and child sit by it: acid rain has erased many of the patterns and it is difficult to make out what they are. Suddenly a great shaft of light from the low sun strikes the stone, and they see ring after ring that was invisible before, opened out for them like a page of an illuminated book. They look up and see moorland after moorland shining clear in the west: they enter new territories.

Whoever walks the moor feels others join her and become at one with her, who yearn to see this world again. Fully restored, she understands the marks on the bone shoulderblade in the moss, she recognises the solid path in the mist, and at the steep incline the rhythm of her stride never fails her. From generation to generation, the mountain hares lie in the same locations. To the wild places each one willingly fulfils her vow of respect.

Those who come down off the moor, they are neither mother nor child, they are not becoming, not perishing. Each is in one piece: the genius of the place completes the human integer.

— Valerie Gillies
Poet and Teacher of Writing in Schools

Crossing

Kathleen Raine

Kathleen Raine is a distinguished poet and champion of culture, with twelve volumes of poetry that have been translated into many languages.

She is a scholar of global renown, and an authority on William Blake and W. B. Yeats. She is known for the journal *Temenos*, and for the creation of the Temenos Academy.

Her last volume of autobiography, *India Seen Afar*, is an eloquent celebration of the timeless wisdom of India.

from The Land Unknown

One day soon after I had gone to Martindale I was scrubbing the stone flags of the larder, on my hands and knees, weighed down by the sense of pursuit; I felt that circumstances were robbing me of my identity, so precarious still, as poet, or as whatever it was I hoped to become. Suddenly, as with the shifting of a *gestalt*, I realized that I was the same person whether scrubbing a floor or writing a poem; that my dignity as a being was in no way dependent upon the role which I had at any moment to assume; for all such roles are merely that, and the person free of them all. I became, from that moment, free of the act; and I have never from that day minded any form of necessary work. Perhaps I have minded too little; to me housework and the like has not been so much a burden as a subtle form of sloth, a temptation to put the less before the more important task. It is all too easy, especially for women, to put the less essential physical task before the more essential intangible work; Martha is always self-righteous in her tyranny over Mary. Thus it was that for so many years, before I permitted myself to write a poem, I would feel compelled to complete all my domestic tasks, even down to darning the last pair of children's socks in my work-basket.

I lived, then, during that summer when France fell, in a state and place where all was radiant with that interior light of which Traherne has written; and beyond the continuous interior illumination of moss and fern, of yellow welsh poppies and water flowing over stones reflecting the glitter of pure light, the warmth of the sun on the stone seat under the yew tree, the scent of young birch leaves and lime blossom, the line of the fells ever changing in sun and shadow, certain moments there were of another kind of consciousness altogether. Such a state has been often enough described: Tennyson said he could enter it at will; Richard Jeffries and others have known it well. 'Nature mysticism' occupies, it may be, a relatively humble place on the ladder of perfection as compared with those states of consciousness attained by saints and sages; but as compared with normal consciousness the difference is as between the world and paradise, if indeed it be not precisely that. Descriptions of one state of consciousness in terms of another must, to those who have not themselves known the experience, always give the impression of being figurative or poetic; so it always must be when, in whatever field, ignorance passes judgement upon knowledge. But those who know are unanimous in reporting that such changes of consciousness are not of degree, but of kind; not some strong emotion or excitement but a clarity in which all is minutely perceived as if by finer sense.

I kept always on the table where I wrote my poems a bowl with different beautiful kinds of moss and lycopodium and long and deeply did I gaze at those forms, and into their luminous smaragdine green. There was also a hyacinth growing in an amethyst glass; I was sitting alone, in an evening, at my table, the Aladdin lamp lit, the fire of logs burning in the hearth. All was stilled. I was looking at the hyacinth, and as I gazed at the form of its petals and the strength of their curve as they open and curl back to reveal the mysterious flower centres with their anthers and eye-like hearts, abruptly I found that I was no longer looking *at* it, but *was* it; a distinct, indescribable, but in no way vague, still less emotional, shift of consciousness into the plant itself. Or rather I and the plant were one and indistinguishable; as if the plant were a part of my consciousness. I dared scarcely to breathe, held in a kind of fine attention in which I could sense the very flow of life in the cells. I was not perceiving the flower but living it. I was aware of the life of the plant as a slow flow or circulation of a vital current of liquid light of the utmost purity. I could apprehend as a simple essence formal structure and dynamic process. This dynamic form was, as it seemed, of a spiritual not a material order, or of a finer matter, or of matter itself perceived as spirit. There was nothing emotional about this experience which was, on the contrary, an almost mathematical apprehension of a complex and organized whole, apprehended *as* a whole. This whole was living; and as such inspired a sense of immaculate holiness. Living form — that is how I can best name the essence or soul of the plant. By 'living' I do not mean that which distinguishes animal from plant or plant from mineral, but rather a quality possessed by all these in their different degrees. Either everything is, in this sense, living, or nothing is; this negation being the view to which materialism continually tends; for lack, as I now knew, of the immediate apprehension of life, as life. The experience lasted for some time — I have no idea how long — and I returned to dull common consciousness with a sense of diminution. I had never before experienced the like, nor have I since in the same degree; and yet it seemed at the time not strange but infinitely familiar, as if I were experiencing at last things as they are, was where I belonged, where in some sense, I had always been and would always be. That almost continuous sense of exile and incompleteness of experience which is, I suppose, the average human state, was gone like a film from sight. In these matters to know once is to know for ever. My mother when she was over eighty confided to me an experience she had had as a girl. 'I have never told anyone before,' she said, 'but I think you will understand.' It was simply that, one day, sitting among the heather near Kielder 'I saw that the moor was alive.' That was all. But I understood that she had seen what I had seen.

— Kathleen Raine
Poet
Extract from *The Land Unknown*
Further Chapters of Autobiography, (pp. 117-120)
Hamish Hamilton, London 1975

Alan Rycroft

Alan Rycroft was born in London in 1957, and went to the University of East Anglia to study English. He has worked as a librarian and is currently teaching English to foreign students.

He has been writing poetry since he was 18, and has collaborated on a number of artistic projects with his friend, Jay Ramsay.

At the Waterfalls
of Spirit

Surprisingly fresh and vital after an interminable eight hours on the snail-paced night train from Madrid, I had arrived in Granada, the ancient cultural capital of Andalucia, southern Spain, early one lucent January morning.

Immediately I felt a deep sense of homecoming, as if I had been there before somehow, though as far as my conscious mind was concerned, I never had. I fell into a state of enchantment, a pleasurable sense of participatory intimacy and oneness with the spirit of the place and with its glowing body of lyrical squares and churches and old stone buildings.

Walking past the medieval university, I came across, apparently quite by chance, an old Gothic monastery dating from the 16th century — San Jeronimo, set well back from the road in a secluded courtyard. I waited twenty minutes for the leisurely Andalucian gatekeeper to open up the building and, on entering, my northern eyes were immediately stunned by the shining orange grove that dazzled in the sun at the centre of the monastic cloisters. The whole atmosphere was so light-drenched, pure and magical it drew me bodily into a bright state of clarity and equanimity.

I then went into a side chapel for a period of meditation before a wall of golden icons. I took out my copy of the *Love-Ananda Gita (The Free Song of Love-Bliss)* I always carried with me on my travels and looked long at the picture of its author, my spiritual teacher Da Love-Ananda (the American born Heart-Master Da Free John).

After some minutes engaged in this feeling contemplation, I sensed a strong energy and presence vibrant and pervasive in the chapel with me. I felt it touch and envelop my body, impalpably probing for the depths of my being. I arose and went out into the cloister — all the time this energized and energizing presence waxed stronger. I entered the monastic refectory, a long white-washed hall with benches and an old wooden table, a dignified place of simplicity, where fortunately I was alone.

This force became so potent, I realized instinctively that I had to surrender to it, that there was no resisting it anyway, for it was far stronger than I. It seemed irrepressibly to descend like an invisible cataract out of the space above my head, a solid, liquid wall of sheer

133

energy. My head was forced downward until I was doubled up, as if compelled to bow. In a couple more minutes my forehead was being pressed to the floor, so I had no alternative but to prostrate myself completely in the manner of the devotees of Allah whose ancient city I was in. For some moments, I just lay there face down on the ground permitting this force to do its work — it seemed like the passing of an eternity and I felt somehow relieved of myself in the awesome embrace of a humbling that consumed me.

And then, just as a group of motley Spanish sailors in bright blue uniforms entered the hall, the energy appeared to depart as suddenly and decisively as it had come and I was able to pick myself up off the floor.

I went out into the cloisters, awe-struck and a little relieved, feeling an unutterable gratitude and a sense of the miracle of wonder. The magnified grace of the Spirit-Power transmitted through the initiatory agency of my Teacher had found me even here, far from home and far from him. My hard and separative heart, at war with its own Help, and addicted to its own independent and prodigal meandering, had been made tender, vulnerable, pulverized by this kathartic presence.

I felt bathed and purified (as in the best, most cleansing 'bath' one could ever have) by these luminous cascades of the Holy Spirit that knows no time nor space and can touch us with eternity in any moment when we surrender to it. It eased my being, as if cartloads of dense, contracting opaque layers of karma had been lifted suddenly and miraculously from my shoulders.

Tears welled in my eyes and I recalled a graceful time when I had felt a similar intensity of Presence while sitting in silent darshan[1] with Heart-Master Da during his visit to Europe in the summer of 1986, when I looked into his eyes and saw, literally, 'no-one' there. They were like open windows into Love's primordial deep, the birthless, deathless infinity of the heart.

The next morning I returned to San Jeronimo, subconsciously, I think, hoping for a repeat experience. For some reason the gatekeeper wouldn't let me in! This was a lesson to me. It has often been my observation that experiences of the spirit arise spontaneously and unexpectedly and not at the beck and call of our seeking and attachment to them (which only serves to block and subtly distort the epiphanies themselves).

And no experience, however mighty or sublime, is conclusive. We who have our heads bowed low at the waterfalls of spirit are baptised by the waters that we may glimpse our true estate and the ultimately numinous nature of reality beyond physical appearance.

Blessed with such openings, after which we so casually and habitually close up again, we have no real choice but to enter the 'fire' (in India, this is called *tapas*). And this fire is the whole life of authentic religious practice, that purifies and opens the being in the cauldron of its service and devotion. So that we may abide more constantly and profoundly in and, ultimately, as that presence of the heart, and be truly enlightened by the light we otherwise only glimpse and yearn for, poignantly and briefly, before the shutters of our minds close us down again.

[1] Traditionally, in India, the contemplation of the Guru in his physical form.

— Alan Rycroft
Poet and English Teacher

Jenny Davis

After a fascinating career raising a family, I decided to read Philosophy and Education at the University of Warwick. There I discovered Plato, Kant and Rudolf Steiner, who further inspired a long-held conviction that life and death are part of the same journey of transformation and change. I trained in yoga, aromatherapy and reflexology.

My research, and an even larger dose of intuition and guidance, led me to found The Eden Centre on Exmoor, North Devon, which emphasizes the relationship between creativity and healing.

In 1991 I collaborated with Jay Ramsay and produced a book of poems, *Journey to Eden*. Now I am working on Jay's 'Chrysalis' education project, that explores the poet within.

For details of workshops and retreats, contact me at –
Eden House
38 Lee Rd
Lynton
DEVON EX 3S 6BS
or ring: 0598 53440

A Sunday in Early October

It was a Sunday in early October. I stepped outside Tocil Flats, my new home for the next twelve months. The air was warm and a hazy autumn sun lit up the campus.

After many years spent nurturing a family, living close to the earth in beautiful Dorset, growing organic vegetables, making sweet smelling bread, tending bees and making tangy yogourt from fresh, unpasteurized milk, my present surroundings were less than inspiring. My eyes took in the ugly library block and my own anonymous block of flats. In the distance I could see the more artistic Art Centre. I turned my back on these mottled relics of 1960's architecture and walked towards green fields and trees.

I mused over my daily exchange of philosophical ideas with 'Skip' Squires: local milkman, farmer, church organist and scout leader whose knowledge of Buddhism, Christianity, western and eastern philosophies, economic theories and the Milk Marketing Boards were second to none. How many farmers like Skip allowed their cows the dignity of dying of old age on their chosen patch — sometimes a dry meadow, sometimes a rambling overgrown hedge?

I followed a footpath down one side of an artificial lake. A couple of well-fed mallards made their way to the side of the lake. I thought of Dorset with its rivers and streams and natural flowing landscape, with names such as Up Heaven and Hell's Bottom where one could harvest an abundance of succulent blackberries, sloes the size of plums, golden rosehips and bucket upon bucket of mushrooms. Yet, here I was standing in the grounds of the University of Warwick, contemplating the next three years studying Philosophy and Education — Coventry only five miles distant and only eighteen miles from heavily industrialized Birmingham!

I lifted my arms towards the sun and started to laugh. I'd made a choice and I felt free. My spirits rose as every blade of grass took on new meaning, every changing leaf became a personal symbol of 'seeing', every tree the tree of life. I could see with greater clarity than ever before.

I realized that thought encompasses all aspects of human growth. Even the ugly buildings were part of the process of learning how to create beauty. Thought is both shadow and light. I'd lived my life close to the soil: my world of children, country, poetry and music; now I was experiencing another dimension. A dimension which I'd hitherto acknowledged in words but which was less heartfelt. Thought: clarity of thought, purity of thought — the balance of wholeness, a true understanding of the part Mind plays in the wholeness of Mind, Body and Spirit. Heart thinking became head thinking became heart searching.

As I sat alone, far from home on a well-placed orderly tree trunk, I opened my well-thumbed Plato's *Republic*. The words came alive with new insight, the people of that long ago Republic were me now. Philosophy had transcended concepts. Thoughts and consciousness melt into and outside time. Every thought signifies a consciousness that burrows deep into our subconscious. Every tree, flower, river, chair, table, lamp, hill and road is that thought — we are thought, God is pure thought.

— Jenny Davis
Founder of the Eden Centre

Jonathan Robertson

Jonathan Robertson was born near Manchester, where, after going to school in the country, he entered the university to study physics, chemistry and mathematics. He graduated in Italian and History of Art, which he taught at Bristol University between 1966–76. He married Claude Forcioli in 1966, and has three children.

In 1976, he resigned from Bristol University to devote himself to photography and join his family in Corsica. In 1986, two years after his divorce, he was appointed Course Director in Photography at Duncan of Jordanstone College of Art in Dundee, where he still teaches. He has exhibited and published photographs and critical writing, in France and Britain.

Primavera

To Valerie

The first time I sat down to try and write about the three weeks, almost twenty-one years ago, during which I lived what Jung has called the *oceanic feeling*, my momentum was diverted by what seemed a magical event. In the warm space of my study, enclosed by the roof, a tortoiseshell butterfly taxied hesitantly across the floor like an aging cloth-winged airplane. In February? Without warning it took off across the room at the same moment as a crow crossed the small rectangle of sky above me. Having searched in vain for a way out to the light it finally chose to land, out of all possible surfaces in the room, on my leg, where it seemed to derive some reassurance from our proximity.

Now, a week later, in another space, eating a pear at the end of the day, I am no nearer a description of those three weeks and the butterfly has been caught by the cat. My difficulty comes from a reluctance to try and reconstruct from the outside an experience which can only be described from within. Living in the moment, able to switch from one course of action to another with neither shame nor regret, I felt like a weathercock, turning with the wind, or a Pooh stick, navigating the rapids with a fluency unfamiliar to human beings.

My ability then to embrace paradox with equanimity was met by my wife with distrust, but by my children with the enthusiasm of recognition reserved for a kindred spirit. Extending my conceptual limits was the most challenging and convincing feature of the experience, which has acted as a beacon for me ever since. Within one month I filled four notebooks with details of my life and convictions regarding its direction. Words became inadequate to capture the compelling immediacy of every complex second, in the seamless flux of

I = space (04.07)
I = form (06.11)
and Jonathan wept (06.08)
Moscow, Good Friday, 12 April 1974

One whole notebook stretched from Good Friday to Easter Sunday, wrestling with the inherited concepts of my spiritual upbringing in a search for my own identity, experienced, joyfully, as missing, believed lost; then found again in a purpose, not a person.

141

I am born to love.
Priddy, 03.30, 13 April 1974.

The liberating absence of temporal continuity shrinks, in description, into a collection of disjointed fragments from which the connecting link, once so self-evident, has been bleached out by time. Playing through extracts from the notebooks, the stylus is liable to leave the groove and bounce across the record in a succession of incomprehensible shrieks. But let's try:

My body is on loan to me. One day it will have to be returned to the soil.

Breathing: *Spirit is very close to breath because of its location in the diaphragm.*

I learnt to control pain in the dentist's chair by concentrating tension in the diaphragm while relaxing all other parts of the body. The same is true, I am told, of controlling menstrual pain and childbirth.

Michelle: *when you have to push you couldn't care whether it's a dog or a toad or a monkey or anything else. You just have to push and get it out of you.*

My mother, after singing songs through the night with her father, as he died, said: dying is just like being born; it's hard work.

Seeing: *With the eyes I can penetrate the soul and unite myself with it because I am not only here but everywhere.*

When I photograph I join the world in me, to me in the world, through light. The world and I flow

as one.

Thinking: *I am no longer the guardian of my body but its witness. I = space with immaterial transparent walls through which I am in the world and the world in me.*

Acting: *I do what I am, which is the world. The world lives me as I observe it.*

Sharing the rhythm of the world allows me to know instinctively where to go, what to do, when to observe, when to act, when to resist, when to persevere, when to abandon. For that is the way. In fusing felt and seen, the world is full of signs and omens. To decide something all

> *I have to do is think of the problem then look around for signs, until a decision is taken.*

Creating:
> *I do not make something which is outside me; rather I am that which I make as it is made. I am that which I see, as it is seen. I am that which I hear, as it is heard. I am all things and no single thing.*

> *Things are done, at last, without thinking; are done, simply, or not done, without the endless internal debate, even while doing them, as to whether (or how) they should be done, or not.*

G.H. Mead: Mind, Self and Society, *Toronto 1934/67, p. 223*

> *If mind is socially constituted, then the field or locus of any given individual mind must extend as far as the social activity or apparatus of social relations which constitutes it extends: and hence that field cannot be bounded by the skin of the individual organism to which it belongs.*

One of the immediate catalysts for the experience was a banal example of the eternal triangle, lived, as though it had never happened before, with a woman who desperately wanted a child and her hitherto sterile husband. Less banal was the apparently inexhaustible sequence of 'coincidences', of time and place, of thought and action, of feeling and perception (as we studied, for example, side by side, Meyerhold's design for *The Magnanimous Cuckold*) and I tried to embrace *him* in my love for *her*.

> *Liliane told me that making love under LSD was cellular, then planetary — a movement from sex to head,* from body to mind.

Yet another catalyst was the certainty, which slowly matured during a week spent between Leningrad and Moscow, that if I persevered, I would be able to see *Composition VII* by Kandinsky, then confined to the reserve collection of the Tretyakov Museum. The administrative difficulties, both ideological and practical, dissolved only when I began to pursue this objective as though my life depended on it, with the calm resolve that comes from sacrificing all else to a single aim.

My frustration and its eventual fulfilment projected me into a realm of experience for which I had had no preparation. I began to live, simultaneously, the intended physiological basis of my own human (as opposed to animal) being, together with the incontrovertible evidence for a common source to all forms of life in the universe.

143

The clarity of mind and purposefulness of body revealed to me the structure of forms and my role as observer and actor within it. It was an exhausting time: every tiny detail of perception claimed significance and demanded integration into a greater whole. I slept little, ate carefully, drank much water. Only my inner clarity kept the doctor's threatened intervention at a distance. But eventually the conflicting demands of family and professional life, with their hierarchies and established patterns of behaviour, restored me to my former social self with his familiar inhibitions and cosy anxieties.

Intermittently over the years I have tried to understand what happened, tried to match written accounts of a similar experience, from a wide range of cultures, to my own. As my spiritual centre has drifted from Christianity towards Chaos theory by way of psychology and perceptual intuition, so St. John of the Cross has been joined by Jung, William James, Herrigel, Thoreau, Mantak Chia and Neil Gunn. Occasional walks in the hills alone, and a week in the desert, have reduced the mental static of urban life sufficiently to allow me to confirm my relation to the land, the wind, the night. When the awareness returns I recognise it through its symptoms: the emptiness of mind, my fingers touching my face as though it were that of another, the contraction in the diaphragm (which the Japanese call the *hara*), the sense of lightness of being which, far from unbearable, is a celebration, of the communion of thought, feeling, action and world.

Alone, in yet another space, with the smell of disinfectant and a dedicated cleaner wielding a mop, I type this out on the word processor, watching the white letters appear like clouds in the deep blue rectangular world. I sense, every now and then, the suspense, the absence of breath, of thought, the expectant vacuum behind the screen which matches my own wait for words.

— Jonathan Robertson
Art Lecturer

Deliverance

Judy de la Hoyde

I was born in Cornwall in the middle of the war, and feel my roots to
be Celtic. I went to boarding school and then Cambridge, where I
read Natural Sciences.

I married shortly after getting my degree and had my daughter
Rachel. We went to India for 3 years, where Hugh was born. On
returning I completed my medical training at St. Thomas's in
London and worked in the Portsmouth/Southampton area for a number of years.

In 1986 I left the NHS, having begun to teach dance – that expanded and I began to work as a Medical Counsellor at the Bristol Cancer
Help Centre. Now I have clients at a clinic and at home. I have
become a doting grandmother and find time to dig my garden in
Bisley, Glos. I need the quiet solitary country life with dark night
skies to balance the intense work with people with cancer.

Storm

It was the first day of the great storms in early 1990. I was to drive from Winchester, where I lived, to Stroud to see a friend. I set off at about 9.30 in the morning, having heard nothing of the forecasted storms. It did seem rather windy and I drove quite slowly. I liked to use the old Roman road from Winchester to Andover through Wherwell. Driving up it, the wind certainly seemed stronger and I slowed down more. The road runs due North, with beech trees several deep on the left hand side for some distance — the wind was coming directly from that side, buffeting the car quite a lot.

Suddenly, after I had gone about half a mile, an enormous beech tree fell across the road about 20 yards straight ahead of me. Then immediately in the mirror, I saw one falling behind me, at about the same distance. Within the next minute or two four more trees fell very close by. The miracle was that my car was beside the only break in the tree line for half a mile in either direction — amidst all the wild fury of the wind and trees falling, I was perfectly safe. I got out of the car and stood watching and listening for a while. The wind seemed to be expressing the fury of the Earth at all the abuse and neglect she has received. As I stood there I heard many more trees falling — mighty trees — toppling like straws in the wind — such devastating destruction all in a few minutes.

I felt completely in awe of the Elements — their ultimate supreme power — and at the same time deeply aware of my safety — the sense of being profoundly cared for. A couple of seconds either way and my car would have been flattened by one of the great beeches.

— Judy de la Hoyde
Doctor

Christopher Kesting-Jiménez

Christopher Kesting-Jiménez was born in York on January 26, 1953. He grew up and went to school in Hastings. In 1976 he graduated in psychology at the University of Sussex.

As an autodidactic multi-media artist in his twenties, he lived, studied, worked and exhibited in Italy, Great Britain, America and Egypt – as a painter, and designer of graphic, interior and festival environments.

In his thirties he lived, studied, worked and exhibited in Great Britain, Spain and Germany – practising artistically applied environmental, architectural and corporate design. In 1987 Christopher married, and is the father of three daughters. Currently he lives in Germany, developing his vocation in artistic psychotherapy, beside his work as art director, design consultant and student of spiritual science.

In the Heart of the Fire

He is present in secret, burning man's heart.

The date is 20th September 1979; and the place is a fifth floor warehouse studio in Canal Street on the lower West side of New York City. It is the early hours of the morning.

Abruptly, I am shocked out of my sleep by a cry: **"Fire! Fire! Fire!"** I leap out of bed and stick my head out of the curtains which separate my corner room from the vast space of the studio. Sure enough there are flames and smoke erupting at the other end, some twenty metres away. Between us, myself and the fire, stands "The Dome of Ancient British Mysteries", a work of environmental art representing six months work for myself and many others. The lights are on. Calmly I step back inside my little sanctuary and reach for the phone. First I raise the emergency services, then I call the owner of the studio, and finally I leave a message at the offices of The Mind, Body and Spirit Festival, the commissioning patron. I have also managed to get my trousers and shoes on. Another peek outside.

Call it naivity or just plain stupidity... all in the moment I realise that the fire has become a raging inferno... and the lights go out. The smoke is suffocating. I close the curtains. In my little corner there is still air to breathe. I am alone, in the pitch of darkness; the tentacles of hell are reaching out for my soul. Beyond the curtain is a being intent on the destruction of my work, and now my life. The struggle is over. The relief after just twenty six years is surprising. Now I can rest again.

Faces begin to flash before my mind's eye; family and friends. There is an ever growing doubt nagging through my ebbing existence. I cannot leave these people. I have not finished my work. There is something I need still to do. I cannot lie down. I must escape.

Shocked back to consciousness, I feel every breath burn my lungs. The heat is threatening to lacerate my flesh. Mortal fear crushes me into submission. I am melting — uncontrolled panic, flowing, fleeing... flying. I step towards the window just outside the curtain, I open it. The cool breeze at once refreshes my hope and heightens in contrast the pain behind me. I climb out, oblivious of the burning frame.

Five stories below me is safety and freedom. Crowds are gathered, watching and fighting. They will help me. I will jump. I will survive.

It is the illusion of despair and dementia; I can no longer perceive the unyielding concrete which awaits my broken body.

Abruptly I am shocked out of my sleep by a cry: "Don't jump!"

Which voice was that which reached my paralytic ears soaring above the height, the noise, the chaos. Crystal clear. I understand!

Turning on my knees, I lower myself over the window ledge. Am I climbing down? My feet are hanging in nothing. Further. I press my fingers onto the brief moulding of the facade below. I am not alone. What I do is not my will. I am held by the resolve of higher being to suffer the extremity of my limbs. The window below me reaches out towards my feet; and swinging, glass is shattered... controlled panic, flowing, fleeing, flying. I am through, in one short breath of life, I am through; landing, standing in the cool dark room below the fire. I am free, back in the world of humankind... and as I step out below into the busy street, I am nothing, I am unknown, I am unseen, I am cold without a shirt, I am pain's torture creeping from the burning fingers that saved my mortal coil. I am, running, seeking succour in the dark night of my soul... alone again.

Yet the memory of that moment is a constant reminder that I am, indeed, not alone. My destiny is meaningful; and the guardians of my spirit life will always urge me onward.

— Christopher Kesting-Jiménez
Painter

Harry Thompson

Harry Thompson was born in Bradford in March 1931, and spent the formative years of his life in Cleckheaton. He attended Whitcliffe Mount Grammar School on a County Minor Scholarship. On leaving school he had a number of jobs, including working in a textile mill. When he was old enough he entered the Royal Navy and saw service in the Far East.

During his service in the Navy he met Oonah, who was to become his good right arm and the mother of their two children. They have now been married over 42 years and have wonderful grandchildren.

After the Royal Navy he joined the City of Bradford Police, and spent 25 years working, most of the time, with fingerprints, photography and forensic evidence. Dealing with the most horrific aspects of life, his daily fare was murder, rape and child abuse. It was against this backdrop that his gift emerged. He was on a police driving course when one of his colleagues complained of a headache. Harry placed his hands on his mate's head. He felt an immense surge of energy pass through him, and his mate's headache disappeared.

Thousands of people have come to Harry seeking help for every kind of illness. After he retired from the Police Service, he worked for the Department of Trading Standards, but as more and more people were seeking his help, he relinquished this responsible job to devote himself to full-time healing.

Martin

Eleven-year old Martin had been receiving treatment for a kidney problem over a period of about six months. His treatment had necessitated a stay in one of the largest hospitals in the area. Quite suddenly a blockage occurred in the blood supply to his brain. He lapsed into deep unconsciousness. Although everything possible was done for him, after a couple of days his parents were told: "the optic nerve has been completely destroyed and if Martin recovers he will be totally blind." It was at this point that I was told of the boy's condition.

You see, John, the boy's father, worked with me. He had heard all the stories about what could happen when bearded Harry became involved. That is involved with someone who was sick or injured. In next to no time I was walking into the small side ward where Martin lay, attached to some kind of equipment. I realised that there were a number of people there with Martin's parents. One of them I recognised as the wife of another colleague from work. I recalled that she was a Nursing Sister and a friend of John's family. I stood alongside Martin's cot. I looked down on the lad and immediately realised how fragile his hold on life was. My intelligent mind told me that nothing could be done.

As quick as this thought made itself known, so in the same second I became aware of the healing force flooding through me. There had to be a reason for my being there. The power of the healing completely took away my breath. I realised that the small room was being completely filled with healing love. I looked at the others there and saw the expressions on their faces changing. They could feel it also. John took me into the corridor. He told me that some of the country's finest paediatricians were taking care of his son. But that things were looking very desperate. He talked about the loss of Martin's sight. How could he tell him that he would never see again? This was one of the questions charging around in my head. That was, of course, if he survived. You see, my policeman's mind had already weighed up the evidence. There wasn't much weight in Martin's favour. The scales seemed set to come down on the side of death. But why, then, had the healing come flooding through so powerfully? My quick mind had the answer. I was being used to comfort Martin's parents and family in this their time of greatest need. I was content to be used for that purpose so went back into the ward. I stood beside the cot and placed a hand on Martin's head. I was at a loss as to what to say or do. You see, Harry Thompson, the man, had no real hope that Martin could possibly survive. I knew he could help people with headaches, bad backs, stress and many other similar problems. This was different. This was life or death. Somehow I found the right words and eventually said my farewells.

The following day I was at work, when one of the inspectors called me over. "When you saw Martin last night, were you working your magic?" he wanted to know. I asked him what he meant. The inspector told me that his wife had been in the ward when I walked in. She had told her husband that as I was standing beside the cot looking down at Martin something happened. A change came over the room. Suddenly everything felt more cheerful and optimistic. She also told him that the feeling had persisted even when I left.

This conversation reaffirmed my original thought that the healing force was using me to help Martin's family. To prepare them for their great loss. You see, I still expected the boy to slip away, but felt that I should continue to visit him, for my gift was needed there.

Later that day I returned to the hospital. I went into the ward and immediately John caught me by the arm and took me out into the corridor. "You knew yesterday, didn't you?" he said. I asked him what he meant. "You knew that he was going to die." It all came pouring out. That afternoon Martin's parents had been told that nothing further could be done. Martin would slowly slip deeper into unconsciousness and eventually pass from this world. I did my best to comfort him and made my way back into the ward. Even today when I tell this story, there is a look of wonderment in my eyes as I describe the sense of power which suddenly came flooding through me. A power which increased in intensity as I approached the cot. I stood there looking down on Martin's pale face and was surprised how shallow his breathing was. I reached out and touched his forehead. Did I sense an awareness in Martin or was it my imagination? My sense of reason told me nothing could be done but some irresistible force kept my hand there, linking the boy so powerfully with the world of the living.

Just as suddenly as the healing had started, so it began to wane. I found that I could move my hand and I came away from the cot side. I spoke with Martin's parents. I don't remember what we talked about. I do recall that there were tears all round, including my own. I continued to visit the hospital and saw Martin slip deeper and deeper in coma.

It was Friday afternoon, vividly imprinted on my mind. I went into the ward and immediately realised things were different. All the equipment had been removed from the cot side. The room seemed suddenly much larger. I felt myself drawn to the cot. As I moved across the room I felt as if all the stops had been pulled out. I felt as if I were plugged into the mains electrics. I reached out and touched Martin. There was very little sign of life. Only by really concentrating could I detect the faintest of chest movement as each shallow breath was drawn into that pale body. Death was no stranger to me. I had seen it many times and been present when others had shuffled off this mortal coil, but never before had I seen anyone so close to death. So close but still clinging to life tenaciously.

The healing began to wane. I turned my attention to Mum and Dad. I remember hugging them both in turn and listening as they told me the administration of all medication had stopped and Martin was just being turned every so often. It was only a matter of time now. A time for watching and waiting. I eventually left the hospital, after mentally saying my own farewell to this brave young man. Martin had fought the good fight, but in my mind the final result was not in doubt.

It was a few hours later and the phone rang at Myrtle Cottage. I answered it and immediately recognised the voice as John's. My immediate thought was, 'He's gone'. Then I realised the voice was real chirpy. He was saying that a miracle had happened. Martin had come out of his coma and was sitting up in bed. Not only had he come back but, wonder of wonders, he could see out of one eye. My first feeling was of absolute joy. This was followed by a deep feeling of betrayal. Me of all people had not believed in the ability of my gift to surmount all these obstacles. But this amazing power had done just that, it had done the impossible and brought Martin back from the very threshold of death. A miracle had taken place and the future had been forged in links of unbreakable steel. I may sum it up very simply: "Martin's recovery was the catalyst that set my attitude for the future. Never, ever again have I limited the power of this wonderful gift of mine by my own human thoughts." A week later, after further healing, Martin recovered the sight in his other eye.

At the time of this writing Martin is in his 18th year. He is six feet tall, weighs somewhere in the region of seventeen stones. His interests vary from archery to the making and flying of radio controlled aircraft. He is a man who will always be so much a part of the life of Harry the Healer.

So many times since that wonderful day I have coaxed my patients into aiming to achieve the highest goal, telling them to aim for the mountain top, never mind just half way up. Some have made the impossible journey against all odds, others have faltered half way to give up on themselves. You see, this gift of mine can do anything and I do mean anything. I never miss a day without remembering the Friday of Martin's recovery. In this remembering I know that with God nothing is impossible.

— Harry Thompson
Healer and ex-Police Officer
Extract from *Just Harry and...*
The Stories of a Natural Healer
by Oonah and Harry Thompson

Helen Yaffe

"And then I left, or call it 'died'"

April 1958 and I had given birth to my last child by Caesarian section; the private hospital was run by nuns. Sister Gabrielle looked after me and we had a wonderful rapport. My family and friends thought of me as a 'shimmering butterfly', full of gaiety and laughter and the joy and happiness of life. I never seemed to think or feel deeply, but drank in sunshine, and felt grateful to be alive and to be allowed to experience the beauty of nature, and creation, and love.

I seemed to recover well and was looking forward to going home with my new child, when quite suddenly, I could not breathe — pulmonary embolism. I knew I would die, and I have never felt more at peace, more wonderfully happy and radiant. But I also knew I *could* breathe, not through my nose, not through my mouth, but through the *whole* of my being. I knew that God was with me, and I knew exactly what to do. Not to move, even to ring my bell, which was inches from me — and my whole being called to Sister Gabrielle to come to me.

Between 12 PM and 2 PM the nuns had their lunch and went to pray in their chapel and I knew that few staff were on duty during that time. And all this happened at lunchtime, my lunch on a tray by me. The knowledge that I could breathe without drawing breath, this absolutely glorious feeling of utter peace, the knowledge that I was surrounded by helping energies, this giving up completely to God's wish, this knowledge that a God existed, that I was so privileged to have this wonderful experience at all, all so utterly new, all this has been with me ever since.

Suddenly the door opened and Sister Gabrielle said: "I was praying in the chapel when I heard you call me. What is the matter?" At the time, this telepathic communication was, of course, taken for granted by both of us. The next thing I remembered was being surrounded by medical and nursing staff and a large oxygen cylinder. I have always had an absolute horror of these cylinders and knew that if a mask was clamped on me, I would die. I knew I wanted no human or artificial help; the conviction continued that this was between my newly found God and myself. I could not talk and had to convey all this to Sister Gabrielle by communication without words, by tuning in to her. And she understood, for I heard her say: "She does not want it."

And then I left, or call it 'died'. Wonderful peace, utter happiness, colours, shapes. I knew my father welcomed me, for though I could not see faces, I knew it was him. He had died when I was a child. I knew I had a choice — to stay or to return; I wanted to stay with all my being but I knew I had to return to my new baby. I heard myself say to my own God: "Please let me go back. I want to stay, but I must look after my baby".

As you see, I was allowed to return. For a week, I had no bodily functions but just lay. I knew I would live, for I had been allowed to return. My lifeline was my husband's hand and his transmission of life energy and love. I had always insisted on holding hands and had always been teased about it. When he had to leave, I lapsed into unconsciousness and pain. Sister Gabrielle nursed me, but all I wanted was her presence and her hands. She spent her off-duty holding my hands. I could not talk; I knew that I could breathe well and I became increasingly conscious of the fact that I was surrounded by my father, by spirits, energies. I was never alone, always completely and safely surrounded and re-assured.

My progress was slow. I think I was so happy with my newfound discoveries of new dimensions, worlds and feelings unknown, and I wondered if, well, I would be thought of as insane. For I now **knew**. My values had changed; my life would now change just as I would now have to search and go on a journey of discovery, in search of knowledge. But for the time being, I could lie in the womb of unconsciousness and in myself and could use the time in feeling, in opening and taking-in.

The next lesson followed quickly: I felt a sudden 'gearchange' in myself and from then onward progress followed. This feeling of a 'gearchange', a sudden push to my Being was so surprising, that I mentioned it to Sister when I could speak again. She informed me that I had been so very ill for so long, that a prayer meeting was arranged for me and it was during that prayer meeting that I felt the push forward. So I was also taught the power of prayer.

I was informed by the consultants that I was regarded as a miracle, or rather that my recovery and the whole period had been so unusual that it had been recorded in a journal. But I never asked any details, for my real work now began — to search, to learn, to discover, to take an entirely different road, to change my life through my knowledge of God and his miracles and work. This was then not easy; in 1958, one did not talk about all this, especially not with my background. How does one describe a search? Especially as it never ever ends. Development never stops; one subject leads to the next. Already, the pattern took shape.

On my return home from hospital, I was weak and prescribed up to nine drugs daily with the result that I became depressed and frustrated. That determined me to get off drugs, back to my natural capabilities, and I looked for a nanny to look after my baby so that I could devote time to get into nature, into the fells and mountains and decrease my daily dose of drugs. Nanny was a Spiritualist, the first person to help me along. Up to then, I had never even known what that word meant. I attended my first service in that circle and talked to a number of members. Eventually, I was introduced to a sensitive who could see auras and was clairvoyant, and it was she who immediately told me that I had been given the gift of healing.

At first, I did not believe her; "Why me?" I asked her. I did not think I deserved to be given that precious gift. She asked me to come to some healing sessions to be given healing myself; to learn to accept. Suddenly, after six sessions, I told her that I would not return to her as I felt like a charged battery and simply wanted to give, to help.

I was called upon almost immediately to help: whilst out shopping I was told that the husband of an acquaintance had died suddenly and, with my shopping basket still on my arm, I went to see the widow. When I saw her eyes, something inside myself overflowed. I simply took her in my arms, asked the rest of her friends for silence and within seconds, utter peace seemed to descend upon her, her features smoothed out, she closed her eyes and went to sleep. Later on in the evening, she phoned to tell me that this was the first sleep and peace she had experienced since her husband's death. After this, I just needed to phone her and give her healing over the phone to help her. This was the beginning of my healing learnings. I simply opened up to God.

— Helen Yaffe
Healer

Stanley Messenger

Stanley Messenger who is in his seventy-ninth year, has to some extent lived his life backwards. He is just now accessing the inner child he never was seventy years ago, when his parents were busy pushing him into the mould of an education, social assumptions and career prospects which had no possible connection with his paralysed inner perceptions. A common enough story in our time, but Stanley is fortunate in having been able to hang on to the thread of his real self and remain in sight of a real world it can live in. To all deprived children he says: 'Hang on to hope, little ones! Your pain is your doorway!'

The Good Death

There is a unique privilege in being able to share in the experiences of those who have died and lived to tell the tale. In our age a large majority of people deny the possibility of this. APICHTID! "A priori it can't happen, therefore it doesn't." The state of mind which denies the possibility of knowing with certainty that consciousness exists beyond the threshold of death will rationalise all such experiences as memories of the vestigial reactions of the dying brain.

Challenged to the limits of their honesty, the majority in our materialistic times will confess that they don't know, and that no honest person can know, whether there is another dimension of reality we can experience beyond the sense world we perceive with our intelligence. They then divide humanity into two groups; those with the courage to profess an honest atheism, with death as the end; and those whose hunger for meaning and the survival of their identity leads them to embrace some form of religion.

Perceptive atheists observing the religious are quite aware that a large increment of so-called religious experience consists of the projection and objectification of pious hopes. They also observe that these projections lead to a whole realm of profound insights and value judgments which they, the atheists, also value. But (they claim), taken far enough, materialistic humanism also leads to a profound emotional and value-creating evolution of consciousness, retaining at the same time an objective honesty which has accepted the finality of death, and so achieving that characteristic ennoblement which results from the admission that the human condition is, in the last resort, tragic.

From within religious experience itself it looks different. It is only the exceptional atheist who is led, often through artistic creation, to inspire others to a high tragic or comic vision of the human condition. Among those who embrace a religion it may appear that a world of inner riches opens up which can transcend the intellectual dishonesty which so often gives birth to it. Passing through the doorway into the authority of Christian, Islamic, or Hindu doctrine one becomes part of a vast family of the children of gods. Each religion in its different way, whether through the endowment of divine grace, or through an understanding of sacrifice and atonement, or on a path of contemplation, or of meditative practice leading to a condition of bliss or nirvana, — each religion in one way or another removes from the individual human being the near intolerable burden of coming to

161

terms on his own with the fact of death, and of his total isolation on the frontier of the utterly unknown and unknowable.

It is the fact of this exemption from the need to struggle alone up to the ultimate frontier of conscious experience, which leads the exceptional, one might say Nietzschean, atheist to regard all religion as essentially trivial. This works both ways, of course, since from the unique heights of contemplative bliss on the religious path, the triviality of a world of humanity which is blind to all dimensions beyond the world of sense, is ultimate.

All paths, it seems, lead back to the overwhelming question. And throughout history, beyond the secular, and beyond the religious dimension equally, this challenge has presented itself, though usually only to the few, as what has been known as the path of initiation.

Essentially, in all its forms, initiation is no more and no less than passing through the gates of death and returning from the experience with something uniquely new to say. Although all initiations have this in common, each initiate becomes in him-or herself transformed into a unique window for others into a transcendental dimension.

So different are the visions of reality which initiates can convey that the paths of development they open up to those on the hither side of the death experience may be just as divisive as are the different religions. Indeed, there is usually an initiate at the foundation point of each religion, and at each branching point as religions divide into their various sects and subdivisions.

The heights of secular or atheistic enlightenment are equally marked by individuals who have transcended the boundaries of ordinary sense-experience, however they may have interpreted this in conceptual or cosmological terms. Ultimately, we are faced, therefore, with a challenge that threatens humanity with total mutual destruction as the different, and probably incompatible certainties of initiate revelation confront one another at a profane level. Christians who have done no more than glimpse the Christ are intent on the utter destruction of Moslems who have no more than glimpsed Allah. And so we approach Armageddon.

It is this which makes the approach of individuals to their own death experience of unique importance in our time, for it is only from this perspective that it is possible to see that beyond the threshold of death truths and visions unique in themselves are no longer mutually incompatible. Peace, one might say, only lies beyond death, but death can already be attained here, on this side of the dissolution of the body. Those who have died and returned, in some unique sense, know that this experience cannot be understood with ordinary intellect, or even with the usual level of heart insight. It has to be 'gone through'. An actual threshold has to be crossed.

In the thirteenth century there was a huge development in southern Europe towards a form of religion which attempted to bring such vision to the ordinary mass of humanity, to bring them within range of initiated insights by living among them in a purified state, and offering them a form of threshold crossing, either during their lives, or at the moment before physical death. This religion was known as Catharism.

It was, of course, a fundamental threat to prevailing forms of religion which wished to exercise religious and political power over the mass of humanity through dogmatic teaching, and the dependency induced by fear-based doctrines of sin, salvation and atonement. So Catharism was extirpated by torture and massacre by the religious and secular authorities, and survived only in small pockets. In a transformed way it has survived in many esoteric cults of the present time, notably in the Rosicrucian stream, and in Anthroposophy.

Catharism was not free from misunderstandings of the nature of reality. In its dualistic theology, it seriously undervalued the spiritual reality of matter and of the Earth itself as the venue and home of the Christ and of Christed humanity. But Catharism sowed the seeds for our time of a healthy relationship to death. It was the aim of the élite group among them, the so-called Perfecti, who had themselves gone through a form of death-initiation, to lead their ordinary believers who could not yet take on board the rigours of a fully purified earth-life, into an experience which they called The Good Death.

The Perfecti had been endowed, through spiritual insight, with a powerful ritual which they called the Consolamentum. This ritual had the effect, as older forms of initiation had, of loosening the spirit-form from the physical body. If this took place during life-experience, it helped to strengthen the grasp on life necessary to live in a very pure and disciplined way. Many individuals could thus take on the responsibilities of Perfecti. But, for the majority, the Consolamentum was given only at the moment of death, which was frequently by torture or burning at the hands of the Inquisition. This enabled them to face death in a somewhat more tolerable way, to replace the fear of an agonizing death with a measure of understanding and insight. To achieve, in other words, a Good Death.

Now, six hundred years later, our bodies and consciousness are different. Many of us are reincarnated Cathars, or have taken part in discoveries about death in other previous lives. Now we live in a time when we need to take a further step in the understanding of the relation of death to life. So we may reach a further crucial threshold on the long road to immortality.

— Stanley Messenger
Thinker and Educator

William Arkle

William Arkle was born in 1924. He trained as an engineer for the Royal Navy during the last war. After this he attended the West of England College of Art to study painting and drawing. His temperament took him in the direction of esoteric and philosophic understanding.

Arkle has produced a book on philosophy called *A Geography of Consciousness,* and a book about his paintings called *The Great Gift.* Recently there have been small books called *Essays* and *The Hologram and Mind.* There are now several tapes of Arkle's music. His paintings, music and writing are about a personal spiritual relationship with God and the re-defining of our understanding of our Creator's purpose.

Letter to the Editor

The Spirit behind such experiences would rather that we managed without them.

I found myself suggesting the above observation about the three categories of special experiences which have been given by Gabriel in relation to thinking, feeling and willing occurrences that changed our lives.

But now I will try to explain the background of thoughts which seemed to prompt me to say such a thing.

Let me start with a feeling I have that as far as our Creator is concerned, the Universe is a university. To be more precise, the Cosmos, at all its levels of being, is a place of learning experience which encourages us to grow to a maximum of maturity; on a par with, but different from Him.

So that when I look at the principles of education I find that the best form that it takes is one in which the learner is virtually unaware of the process. To put it another way, the student is best served by a growth or learning situation when unaware that growth or learning is the objective.

The fruit of learning, in the deepest sense, must be the ability to assess every situation as part of a value system which is the most valuable and beautiful that we can possibly be aware of.

As we become wise, and those who trouble to read this would be such persons, we find that our Creator's value system is the most beautiful one available. Our experience of its beauty causes us to give it great worth and wonder. Our education eventually explains to us how it has been arrived at. Thus our gift from the Creator is the individuality of our Being and the classrooms and playgrounds of creation which enable us to engage in a process of fuller and fuller understanding.

The place in our nature where this understanding occurs is necessarily the deepest place within us. This deepest place is at the centre of the Being nature we are given and is sometimes described as a Spark from the Divine Flame of the Creator's Being. (Capital letters to give such words their greatest value.) Such understanding is only possible as a result of diverse and opposite experiences coming to us which present very many possible 'tastes' surrounding each category or subject on the value list we build for ourselves.

165

Because such a delicate balance is required to assess the 'tastes' from each direction in order to know which 'taste' feels best to this central judge, the process must take place in a condition of tranquillity and without external pressure of any sort. Only then are we our own Person. Only then are we fully valuable to the other Persons, and no less worthy objective could be the cause of the gift from the Creator we come to know.

Now it seemed to me that quite often, and perhaps nearly always, the sort of experiences the three categories are looking at are the result of the proper educational system breaking down. So that here on Earth we are observing a classroom which is suffering from disruption. Ours is an emergency situation where souls are drowning in heavy devaluing influences and therefore requiring special life-saving methods to bring about recovery. Such emergency methods require powerful and sometimes shocking techniques, and my feeling is that such happenings come to us as special experiences.

In so doing, such experiences disable the innermost assessments of tranquillity at the core of our Being and substitute strong and emphatic 'statements' which may well re-activate our engines of will and feeling and thinking, but at the same time create forms of bias and programming which later have to be gentled and balanced.

The best education creeps up on us without us being aware that it is happening. It is in a spirit of zest, enjoyment and deep interest. The worst form is that of the brass band playing man-made music which drowns out the string quartet playing the Creator's music.

So it may be prudent not to begin to equate special experiences with signs of progress so much as signs of difficulty and hesitation in ordering our world and understanding from that place of innermost knowing. Then our wisdom finds that all values depend on the richness and fullness of a very wide and deep curriculum through which the holistic rebound of the smallest and least significant happening is a necessary matrix for the proper valuation of those things that come to find the top places on our list of values.

It is said that the seat of the 'I' is in the heart, thus bringing categories 3 and 2 together. And with the proper working of the mindfulness of the heart, category 1 will join them, and the mindfulness of the head will then take its proper place and look to serve and define the heart.

The sickness among us on earth is the closing of the heart through fear and distrust. But there still exists a great paradox which may cheer us, and that is the equation which understands how to view and value the journey of the prodigal son and the recovery of the soul from a phase of rebellion. But that is the start of another great story.

I also feel that there are very wonderful special experiences that come to us in order to establish, in a form of sublime synthesis, the many different ways that we have been working at the knowing of ourselves. These experiences are to confirm what has gone before rather than to direct what is to come in the future. So, in this way, they do not fit into the definition that they changed our lives.

In a healthier classroom we should not have lost the awareness that everything signified something, our hearts would never have closed, and we would never have lost confidence in the reality or value of our 'I'.

However, I am aware that there are special experiences which do not upset the delicate balance of our innermost taste buds, and that they are a proper part of a healthy orientation and spiritual growth encounters which affect the present and future and even the past.

— William Arkle
Visionary Painter

Enough

Enough. These few words are enough.
If not these words, this breath.
If not this breath, this sitting here.

This opening to the life
we have refused
again and again
until now.

Until now.

— David Whyte
Where Many Rivers Meet 1990
reprinted by kind permission of
Many Rivers Press, Langley WA, USA

If you have difficulties ordering from a bookshop you can order direct from

Hawthorn Press,
Hawthorn House,
1 Lansdown Lane,
Lansdown,
Stroud,
Glos.
United Kingdom,
GL5 1BJ

Telephone 01453 757040
Fax   01453 751138